READER'S GUIDE

TO

The Scarlet Letter

READER'S GUIDE

TO

The Scarlet Letter

Selected and Edited by

Nancy Carr

Joseph Coulson

and

Steve Hettleman
Department of English, Redwood High School
Larkspur, California

Published by the Great Books Foundation
A nonprofit educational organization

Published and distributed by

The Great Books Foundation
A nonprofit educational organization

35 East Wacker Drive, Suite 2300
Chicago, IL 60601-2298
www.greatbooks.org

First printing
9 8 7 6 5 4 3 2 1 0

⊗This paper meets the requirements of
ANSI/NISO Z39.48-1992 (Permanence of Paper).

Library of Congress Cataloging-in-Publication Data

Reader's guide to The scarlet letter / selected and edited
by Nancy Carr, Joseph Coulson, and Steve Hettleman.
     p. cm.
  Includes bibliographical references.
  ISBN 1-880323-89-3 (alk. paper)
   1. Hawthorne, Nathaniel, 1804–1864. Scarlet letter. 2. Historical fiction,
American—History and criticism. 3. Mothers and daughters in literature.
4. Massachusetts—In literature. 5. Puritans in literature. 6. Adultery in literature.
7. Women in literature. I. Carr, Nancy. II. Coulson, Joseph. III. Hettleman, Steve.
IV. Great Books Foundation (U.S.)

PS1868 .R37 2003
813'.3—dc21
                                     2002190705

Book cover and interior design:
William Seabright & Associates

About the Great Books Foundation

What is the Great Books Foundation?

The Great Books Foundation is an independent, nonprofit educational organization whose mission is to help people learn how to think and share ideas. Toward this end, the Foundation offers workshops in shared inquiry discussion and publishes collections of classic and modern texts for both children and adults.

The Great Books Foundation was established in 1947 to promote liberal education for the general public. In 1962, the Foundation extended its mission to children with the introduction of Junior Great Books. Since its inception, the Foundation has helped thousands of people throughout the United States and in other countries begin their own discussion groups in schools, libraries, and community centers. Today, Foundation instructors conduct hundreds of workshops each year, in which educators and parents learn to lead shared inquiry discussion.

What resources are available to support my participation in shared inquiry?

The Great Books Foundation offers workshops in shared inquiry to help people get the most from discussion. Participants learn how to read actively, pose fruitful questions, and listen and respond to others effectively in discussion. All participants also practice leading a discussion and have an opportunity to reflect on the process with others. For more information about Great Books materials or workshops, call the Great Books Foundation at 1-800-222-5870 or visit our Web site at www.greatbooks.org.

The Great Books Foundation

Contents

Introduction

More than 150 years after its initial publication, Nathaniel Hawthorne's *The Scarlet Letter* remains one of the most widely read American novels. On the surface, our world today could not be more different than the one inhabited by Hester Prynne, Arthur Dimmesdale, and Roger Chillingworth. Almost all of North America has been explored and settled. There is a greater separation between church and state. Citizens with very different ideas about what is moral and immoral live side by side. So what is it about *The Scarlet Letter* that remains relevant? Perhaps we admire Hester's dignity in the face of ostracism or sympathize with Dimmesdale's inability to do what he knows needs to be done. Perhaps we learn something about revenge from observing the single-minded Chillingworth. Or perhaps the rigid beliefs and the harsh judgments of the Puritans remind us that there is a fine line between religious fervor and fanaticism.

yes - but debatable if we are going back to less?

whether it be Osama bin laden or the religious right.

The Great Books Foundation has created this Reader's Guide in an effort to support careful reading and discussion of *The Scarlet Letter.* Here we provide open-ended questions—for the novel as a whole and for individual chapters—that offer many opportunities for interpretation. We believe that good questions require close reading and active thinking; we also believe that answers should be backed up with evidence from the text. Thought-provoking discussions that ask for close attention to the text will lead to a deeper understanding of this important novel.

Because Puritan New England was so different from our contemporary world, we have also provided a range of background materials that make Hawthorne's and Hester's worlds more familiar. We have included an author biography, two of Hawthorne's short stories, a series of articles and essays that place the novel and its author in their historical contexts, a glossary of literary terms, and a bibliography with resources for further reading.

It is our hope that you find this encounter with *The Scarlet Letter,* whether it is your first or fifth such encounter, a rewarding one.

About Shared Inquiry

Shared inquiry is the effort to achieve a more thorough understanding of a text by discussing questions, responses, and insights with others. For both the leader and the participants, careful listening is essential. The leader guides the discussion by asking questions about specific ideas and problems of meaning in the text, but does not seek to impose his or her own interpretation on the group.

During a shared inquiry discussion, group members consider a number of possible ideas and weigh the evidence for each. Ideas that are entertained and then refined or abandoned are not thought of as mistakes, but as valuable parts of the thinking process. Group members gain experience in communicating complex ideas and in supporting, testing, and expanding their thoughts. Everyone in the group contributes to the discussion, and while participants may disagree with each other, they treat each other's ideas respectfully.

This process of communal discovery is vital to developing an understanding of important texts and ideas, rather than merely cataloging knowledge about them. By reading and thinking together about important works, you and the other members of your group are joining a great conversation that extends across the centuries.

Guidelines for leading and participating in discussion

Over the past fifty years, the Great Books Foundation has developed guidelines that distill the experience of many discussion groups, with participants of all ages. We have found that when groups follow the procedures outlined below, discussions are most focused and fruitful.

1. **Read the selection before participating in the discussion.** This ensures that all participants are equally prepared to talk about the ideas in the work, and helps prevent talk that would distract the group from its purpose.

2. **Support your ideas with evidence from the text.** This keeps the discussion focused on understanding the selection and enables the group to weigh textual support for different answers and to choose intelligently among them.

3. **Discuss the ideas in the selection, and try to understand them fully before exploring issues that go beyond the selection.** Reflecting on a range of ideas and the evidence to support them makes the exploration of related issues more productive.

4. **Listen to others and respond to them directly.** Shared inquiry is about the give-and-take of ideas, a willingness to listen to others and to talk to them respectfully. Directing your comments and questions to other group members, not always to the leader, will make the discussion livelier and more dynamic.

5. **Expect the leader to ask questions, rather than answer them.** The leader is a kind of chief learner, whose role is to keep discussion effective and interesting by listening and asking questions. The leader's goal is to help the participants develop their own ideas, with everyone (the leader included) gaining a new understanding in the process. When participants hang back and wait for the leader to suggest answers, discussion falters.

How to make discussions more effective

- **Ask questions when something is unclear.** Simply asking someone to explain what he or she means by a particular word, or to repeat a comment, can give everyone in the group time to think about the idea in depth.

- **Ask for evidence.** Asking "What in the text gave you that idea?" helps everyone better understand the reasoning behind an answer, and it allows the group to consider which ideas have the best support.

- **Ask for agreement and disagreement.** "Does your idea agree with hers, or is it different?" Questions of this kind help the group understand how ideas are related or distinct.

- **Reflect on discussion afterward.** Sharing comments about how the discussion went and ideas for improvement can make each discussion better than the last.

Room arrangement and group size

Ideally, everyone in a discussion should be able to see and hear everyone else. When it isn't possible to arrange the seating in a circle or horseshoe, encourage group members to look at the person talking, acknowledging one another and not just the leader.

In general, shared inquiry discussion is most effective in groups of ten to twenty participants. If a group is much bigger than twenty, it is important to ensure that everyone has a chance to speak. This can be accomplished either by dividing the group in half for discussion or by setting aside time at the end of discussion to go around the room and give each person a chance to make a brief final comment.

Using the Reader's Guide

"The Minister's Black Veil" and "Ethan Brand" by Nathaniel Hawthorne

"The Minister's Black Veil" and "Ethan Brand" were chosen for their thematic connections to *The Scarlet Letter*. Using the questions provided, readers can discuss these stories apart from the novel or as an introduction to some of the novel's ideas and themes. Discussing the stories either before or after reading the novel provides an excellent opportunity for comparative analysis.

Interpretive Questions for Discussion of *The Scarlet Letter*

Discussion gives participants of all ages an opportunity to express their ideas, listen to the perspectives of others, and synthesize different viewpoints to reach a deeper, more informed understanding of the novel. Effective questions help participants talk specifically about the content and language of the novel, arrange details in logical order, and support their ideas with evidence from the text and personal experience.

Passages and Questions for Close Reading

Passages from *The Scarlet Letter* and related questions can be discussed in large and small groups or can be used for individual study and written response. The questions ask the reader to analyze specific literary themes, techniques, and terms as part of the interpretive process.

All readers will benefit from the challenges these questions pose. *Students in honors courses or courses qualifying for college credit will find these questions useful for exam preparation.*

Suggestions for Writing

Postdiscussion writing gives students the opportunity to consider new ideas and measure them against their personal experience and opinions. In these extended writing pieces, students can return to questions not fully resolved in discussion or investigate unexplored avenues of inquiry. Because thorough discussion requires such extensive engagement with the novel, students are better prepared to present their ideas clearly and persuasively or, in the more creative writing assignments, to produce a more fully imagined response.

Background and Context

These selections place the novel and its author in their historical context. Documents about Puritan New England and the Salem witchcraft trials, along with notes concerning the origins of the novel, give readers a clearer understanding of Hawthorne's inspiration. Reviews and essays reveal how *The Scarlet Letter* has been received since it was first published.

When used in the classroom, these selections invite teachers and students in English and history to join forces in discussion of *The Scarlet Letter*, examining the social, cultural, and political climate from which the novel emerged.

Footnotes by the author are not bracketed; footnotes by the Great Books Foundation, an editor, or a translator are [bracketed].

READER'S GUIDE

TO

The Scarlet Letter

About the Author

Sin, secrecy, guilt: these are the themes that Nathaniel Hawthorne repeatedly explores in his fiction. As a person, Hawthorne was circumspect and reserved, and his introspection and need for privacy imbued his life with an air of mystery, making him something of an enigma even to his family and close friends. After his death, his wife, Sophia, wrote that she "never dared gaze at him unless his lids were down. It seemed an invasion into a holy place—To the last he was in a measure to me a divine Mystery, for he was so to himself." This sense of an ultimately inaccessible self runs throughout Hawthorne's life and his fiction.

Hawthorne's fascination with the hidden dimensions of human character is in part a reflection of his Puritan heritage. Born in 1804 in Salem, Massachusetts, Hawthorne was descended from the Hathornes, who had been prominent in Salem since colonial times. One of Hawthorne's ancestors, John Hathorne, was a judge at the notorious witchcraft trials of the 1690s. Particularly disturbing to Hawthorne was the fact that his ancestor, unlike most of his Puritan colleagues, never repented of his part in the trials. Given this family history, Hawthorne was deeply ambivalent about his birthplace, repeatedly leaving Salem throughout his life only to return to it. For Hawthorne, the Puritan past, with its emphasis on secret sin and its intolerance of human frailty, was a source of both pain and inspiration.

Hawthorne's own early history also had its darker passages. His father, a ship's captain, died when Hawthorne was four, and he and his sisters were raised by his mother and her family. Later in life, Hawthorne traced his habit of retreating into solitude to his childhood, when a leg injury kept him at home from the age of nine to eleven. Biographers have differed about whether this injury was physical or psychological, but it is clear that Hawthorne preferred staying at home, reading, and making up his own stories to attending school. He read a wide range of authors, including John Bunyan, Michel de Montaigne, Jean Jacques Rousseau, William Shakespeare, and Edmund Spenser. He began writing essays and poems at an early age, and for a time edited a newspaper for his family, writing all the articles himself.

It was at Bowdoin College that Hawthorne made his first close friendships and formed the firm ambition to become a writer. He was a strikingly handsome young man, and though he could be silent and reserved, his friends considered these characteristics part of his charm. In 1821, when he entered Bowdoin, its enrollment was 108 students, with a freshman class of 38. The small class size fostered strong relationships, and Hawthorne made two friends he would remain close to throughout his life: future U.S. president Franklin Pierce and Horatio Bridge, who became a career Navy officer and also wrote nonfiction. While at college, Hawthorne spent a great deal of his time gambling, drinking, cutting classes and study periods, and writing fiction. He knew that it would be extremely difficult to earn a living as a writer, and, after graduation in 1825, he returned to his mother's family in Salem.

For the next twelve years, Hawthorne concentrated on becoming a published writer, shutting himself into a room on an upper floor for days at a time. Writing in a room with a view on an upper floor would be his practice for the rest of his life. Hawthorne later described himself as a virtual hermit during this time in Salem, but, in reality, he frequented taverns and had a circle of friends among the Salem Democrats, who came from a more mixed social class than did the Whigs. The Democratic Party was the party of Pierce and Bridge, and Hawthorne remained loyal to it all his life.

But Hawthorne's writing apprenticeship in Salem was also a time of mental anguish. In 1828, Hawthorne published his first novel, *Fanshawe*. It was published anonymously, a common practice at the time. Set at a New England college, the novel was partly autobiographical. The book received some favorable reviews, but, a few years after its publication, Hawthorne became so ashamed of it that he asked his friends to burn their copies, and later never told his wife of its existence. He also burned the manuscript of *Seven Tales of My Native Land*, his first collection of stories, and today only two tales survive. In the early 1830s, Hawthorne began publishing stories in periodicals such as the *Token, Salem Gazette,* and *New-England Magazine.* The pay was far too low for him to live on, ranging from nothing to a dollar per published page. In 1836, at the age of thirty-two, Hawthorne was greatly discouraged. So far he had no indication he would ever earn money or renown as an author.

The next year, Hawthorne's fortunes began to improve. He published the collection *Twice-Told Tales,* which included his finest work to date. "The May-Pole of Merry Mount," "The Gentle Boy," and "The Minister's Black Veil" rank with the best fiction he was to write. The book received some good reviews, including one by the poet Henry Wadsworth Longfellow. Just as important, Hawthorne met his future wife, Sophia Peabody, that same year.

Sophia was to have a profound influence on Hawthorne's life, despite the ambiguous beginning of their relationship and their long, ambivalent (on Hawthorne's part) engagement. Sophia came from a well-to-do, socially progressive family with abolitionist sympathies. At first it was unclear whether Hawthorne was more attracted to Sophia's sister Elizabeth or to Sophia, and their courtship was long and indirect. At one point, Hawthorne dallied with a local beauty known as "The Star of Salem," but the relationship ended when she demanded that Hawthorne fight a duel to defend her honor. Sophia, however, was sure of her own feelings and waited patiently for Hawthorne to clarify his. About a year after their meeting, in 1839, they were engaged, but Hawthorne waited several years before telling his family.

Hawthorne had a number of reasons for keeping the engagement secret. He hoped to be earning more money before marrying, he was

Hawthorne's children, Una, Julian, and Rose, circa 1862

concerned about the probable reaction of his and Sophia's families to the news, and he was unsure about giving up his bachelor existence. At this point in Hawthorne's life, an experimental community called Brook Farm appealed strongly to him.

Hawthorne joined Brook Farm, located outside Boston, in 1841. Life in the community was to be based on the principles of transcendentalism, a literary and philosophical movement that became strongly identified with New England authors and intellectuals like Bronson Alcott, Ralph Waldo Emerson, and Henry David Thoreau. Transcendentalists believed that human beings were

Brook Farm (1844), by Josiah Wolcott. This idealized landscape belies the harsh reality of manual labor that Hawthorne discovered while living in this experimental community.

basically good and emphasized individual conscience, living in harmony with nature, and the compatibility of manual labor and intellectual work. Hawthorne bought two shares in the community, at $500 each, and invested an additional $500, at a time when he was earning about $1,500 a year. Though he was to stay at Brook Farm for less than a year, the experience was important in his development as a writer. There he was introduced to some in the transcendentalist circle, including Margaret Fuller and William Ellery Channing, and he based *The Blithedale Romance* (1852) on his experiences at the farm.

In a matter of months, Hawthorne became convinced that the farm would never support itself, and he formally resigned in October 1842. Earlier in 1842, Sophia had at last brought Hawthorne to tell their families of their engagement. Their families' reactions more than justified Hawthorne's hesitation: the news caused emotional upheavals that took some time to die down. But in July 1842, he and Sophia were married, and the happiest and most productive period of Hawthorne's life began.

The newlyweds moved to Concord, Massachusetts, where they rented the Old Manse (minister's house), which had been built by William Emerson, Ralph Waldo Emerson's grandfather. In 1836, Ralph Waldo Emerson had written *Nature,* one of the founding texts of transcendentalism, at the Manse. With its proximity to the Concord River, its fruit orchard, and its large garden, the house was a kind of paradise for the young couple. Sophia refurbished the house and lavished special attention on Hawthorne's second-floor study. Together, she and Hawthorne marked their residence by etching words on the window panes of the study with Sophia's diamond ring. The window, which can still be seen in the house today, reads "Man's accidents are God's purposes / Sophia A. Hawthorne 1843" and "Nath^L Hawthorne / This is his study. / 1843 . . . / The smallest twig / leans clear against the sky. Composed by my wife and written with her diamond." Sophia added "Inscribed by my husband at sunset / April 3rd 1843 / In the gold light. SAH." In this study, Hawthorne wrote the tales in *Mosses from an Old Manse* (1846), the last short-story collection he was to publish. It includes several of his most powerful stories, among them "The Birth-Mark" and "Rappaccinni's Daughter."

While living at the Old Manse, Hawthorne associated with the most important writers of the transcendentalist movement. Emerson came to visit, but he and Hawthorne did not become friends. Though evidence is scanty, they seem not to have admired each other's writing. Emerson felt that Hawthorne's fiction lacked "a purer power," while Hawthorne found Emerson's writing too ethereal, too much a part of the "cloud-land" he thought the transcendentalists generally inhabited. Henry David Thoreau and Hawthorne got along better. They went sailing on the Concord River, and in their writings expressed a qualified admiration for each other. Both intensely private men, they remained acquaintances rather than friends.

The Old Manse idyll ended in 1845, when finances forced the Hawthornes to return to Salem. Their family was growing: they moved back to Salem with a two-year-old daughter, Una, and Julian was born in 1846. Under U.S. President James K. Polk, a Democrat, Hawthorne's friends had enough influence to get him a post at the Salem Custom House, a position he kept for three years.

In 1849, Hawthorne suffered two major losses, and out of this time of great anger and grief came his acknowledged masterpiece, *The Scarlet Letter*. First Hawthorne was ousted from his job at the Custom House for political reasons, and, in late July of the same year, his mother died. Hawthorne immediately began planning to leave Salem, and he arranged to move to Lenox, Massachusetts, in March 1850. Between August 1849 and February 1850, Hawthorne wrote *The Scarlet Letter*, working at almost frantic speed. He had planned to make it part of a collection of tales, but his publisher recommended letting *The Scarlet Letter* stand alone. Only "The Custom House" remains of Hawthorne's original plan.

Despite Hawthorne's fears that *The Scarlet Letter* was too dark to be popular, the first edition of 2,500 copies sold out within ten days. Some reviewers were shocked by the subject matter and disapproved of what they took to be Hawthorne's lax moral tone, but the book was almost immediately recognized as a classic. Hawthorne's literary reputation was made. The people of Salem were furious about his depiction of the Custom House, but Hawthorne refused to alter the sketch and inserted a preface in the book's second edition restating its accuracy.

Once in Lenox, Hawthorne became part of a literary social circle that included Oliver Wendell Holmes, and the group went on frequent excursions. During one of these trips, Hawthorne met Herman Melville. So began an emotionally charged friendship of great importance, particularly to Melville, even though the two men saw each other only rarely after the friendship's early days.

The friendship began, appropriately enough, with writing. After his initial meeting with Melville, Hawthorne wrote to Horatio Bridge about his liking for the young author (fifteen years Hawthorne's junior), and Melville published an unsigned, glowing review of *Mosses from an Old Manse*. From the beginning, Melville pursued the friendship more strongly than Hawthorne, setting up their meetings and taking responsibility for staying in contact. To Melville, Hawthorne was both a father figure and the one friend who seemed to understand his literary aspirations. Melville revised and expanded the draft of *Moby-Dick* after meeting Hawthorne, and dedicated the book to him when it was published. In a letter, he told Hawthorne that he felt "the Godhead is broken up like the bread at the Supper, and that we are the pieces. Hence this infinite fraternity of feeling." Faced with such ardently expressed admiration, Hawthorne, always wary of intimacy, backed away. Though the two authors continued to correspond occasionally, they never again met so often or were so close.

Hawthorne's wife, Sophia Peabody Hawthorne (1809–1871), from a portrait painted in 1846. Sophia was herself a writer and also an artist. She illustrated Hawthorne's "The Gentle Boy: A Thrice-Told Tale" and edited his notebooks for publication.

During the early 1850s, Hawthorne was publishing his most important works. In addition to *The Scarlet Letter*, these included *The House of the Seven Gables, A Wonder-Book for Girls and Boys, The Snow-Image, and Other Twice-Told Tales,* and *The Blithedale Romance.* It was in 1851, twenty-six years after he began trying to be a professional writer, that he finally earned enough from writing to support his family. The Hawthornes now had three children; a second daughter, Rose, was born in 1851.

The intense literary activity of the Lenox period came to an end in 1852, when the Hawthornes bought Bronson Alcott's house in Concord and some acreage from Ralph Waldo Emerson. Hawthorne's next writing project was a biography of his old friend Franklin Pierce, who was now running for U.S. president. When Pierce was elected, Hawthorne was appointed consul for

Liverpool. The post paid well and enabled the family to live and travel abroad. But the mid-1850s were the beginning of Hawthorne's literary decline, and some biographers believe that the deterioration of his health, manifested by restlessness and weakness, also began then.

In 1856, Hawthorne and Melville had a gloomy meeting; both were discouraged about the public's inability to appreciate challenging and innovative writing. Melville was deeply depressed about the lukewarm reception of his recent novels, including *Moby-Dick*. Hawthorne, for his part, bitterly resented the great popular success of some women writers of the time. Some of these, like E. D. E. N. Southworth, are practically forgotten today; others, like Harriet Beecher Stowe, are newly appreciated in our own time. In a letter, Hawthorne complained that "America is now wholly given over to a d——d mob of scribbling women, and I should have no chance of success while the public taste is occupied with their trash—and should be ashamed of myself if I did succeed." Hawthorne's frustration stemmed from both the critical reception of his later works—none of which were as popular or well-regarded as *The Scarlet Letter*—and from his ongoing struggles with his writing.

The Marble Faun, Hawthorne's last completed novel, appeared in 1860. It was set in Rome, where the family had been living, and Sophia later blamed her husband's physical decline in part on this time in Italy. Certainly Hawthorne was anxious about his daughter Una's health; she was quite ill in 1858, probably with malaria, and was never again fully well.

Returning to Concord—particularly to the literary group that included the Alcotts, Thoreau, and Emerson—revived Hawthorne's spirits somewhat. He added a tower to the Concord house, modeling it on the tower he had written in while in Rome. Though he began new novels, he was to publish only *Our Old Home*, a nonfiction account of his experiences in England.

Hawthorne was already dispirited when the Civil War broke out in 1861, and his mixed feelings about the war increased his anxiety and misery. He thought the North and South should separate for good and could not imagine the war ending with a restored Union. He wrote to Horatio Bridge, "I don't quite understand what we are fighting for, or what definite result can be expected." By the end of 1863, Hawthorne was obviously ill. He had lost a great deal of weight, was tired and restless, and suffered from fainting spells. He was making no progress on his writing. Since he steadfastly refused to see a doctor, his illness was never diagnosed.

In early 1864, at age sixty, Hawthorne was increasingly feeble and had trouble walking; he admitted feeling "boring pain, distention, difficult digestion." Nevertheless, in May of that year, he agreed to take a trip through the New England countryside with Franklin Pierce. They set off on May 12 but made halting progress, due to Hawthorne's weakness. On May 18, they reached Plymouth, New Hampshire. Alarmed by Hawthorne's condition, Pierce planned to write to Sophia the next day and take Hawthorne no further. Early on May 19, Hawthorne died in his sleep at the inn.

Hawthorne was buried in Concord's new Sleepy Hollow Cemetery, where he was later surrounded by his old associates Thoreau, Emerson, and the Alcotts. In 1891, Melville published his long poem "Monody," which clearly addresses his friendship with Hawthorne. Melville wrote of his sorrow: "To have known him, to have loved him /After loneness long; /And then to be estranged in life, /And neither in the wrong." Hawthorne would have appreciated the sentiment, feeling as he did the inescapable isolation of each human being.

Nathaniel and Sophia Hawthorne (bottom left) at the Wayside, their Concord home, after the addition of the tower studio.

This story was published in the *Token* in 1836,
fourteen years before *The Scarlet Letter*.

The Minister's Black Veil

A Parable[*]

Nathaniel Hawthorne

The sexton stood in the porch of Milford meetinghouse, pulling lustily at the bell-rope. The old people of the village came stooping along the street. Children, with bright faces, tript merrily beside their parents, or mimicked a graver gait, in the conscious dignity of their Sunday clothes. Spruce bachelors looked sidelong at the pretty maidens, and fancied that the Sabbath sunshine made them prettier than on weekdays. When the throng had mostly streamed into the porch, the sexton began to toll the bell, keeping his eye on the Reverend Mr. Hooper's door. The first glimpse of the clergyman's figure was the signal for the bell to cease its summons.

"But what has good Parson Hooper got upon his face?" cried the sexton in astonishment.

All within hearing immediately turned about, and beheld the semblance of Mr. Hooper, pacing slowly his meditative way toward the meetinghouse. With one accord they started, expressing more wonder than if some strange minister were coming to dust the cushions of Mr. Hooper's pulpit.

"Are you sure it is our parson?" inquired Goodman Gray of the sexton.

"Of a certainty it is good Mr. Hooper," replied the sexton. "He was to have exchanged pulpits with Parson Shute of Westbury; but Parson Shute sent to excuse himself yesterday, being to preach a funeral sermon."

---

[*] Another clergyman in New England, Mr. Joseph Moody, of York, Maine, who died about eighty years since, made himself remarkable by the same eccentricity that is here related of the Reverend Mr. Hooper. In his case, however, the symbol had a different import. In early life he had accidentally killed a beloved friend; and from that day till the hour of his own death, he hid his face from men.

The cause of so much amazement may appear sufficiently slight. Mr. Hooper, a gentlemanly person of about thirty, though still a bachelor, was dressed with due clerical neatness, as if a careful wife had starched his band, and brushed the weekly dust from his Sunday's garb. There was but one thing remarkable in his appearance. Swathed about his forehead, and hanging down over his face, so low as to be shaken by his breath, Mr. Hooper had on a black veil. On a nearer view, it seemed to consist of two folds of crape, which entirely concealed his features, except the mouth and chin, but probably did not intercept his sight, farther than to give a darkened aspect to all living and inanimate things. With this gloomy shade before him, good Mr. Hooper walked onward, at a slow and quiet pace, stooping somewhat and looking on the ground, as is customary with abstracted men, yet nodding kindly to those of his parishioners who still waited on the meetinghouse steps. But so wonder-struck were they, that his greeting hardly met with a return.

"I can't really feel as if good Mr. Hooper's face was behind that piece of crape," said the sexton.

"I don't like it," muttered an old woman, as she hobbled into the meetinghouse. "He has changed himself into something awful, only by hiding his face."

"Our parson has gone mad!" cried Goodman Gray, following him across the threshold.

A rumor of some unaccountable phenomenon had preceded Mr. Hooper into the meetinghouse, and set all the congregation astir. Few could refrain from twisting their heads toward the door; many stood upright, and turned directly about; while several little boys clambered upon the seats, and came down again with a terrible racket. There was a general bustle, a rustling of the women's gowns and shuffling of the men's feet, greatly at variance with that hushed repose which should attend the entrance of the minister. But Mr. Hooper appeared not to notice the perturbation of his people. He entered with an almost noiseless step, bent his head mildly to the pews on each side, and bowed as he passed his oldest parishioner, a white-haired great-grandsire, who occupied an armchair in the center of the aisle. It was strange to observe, how slowly this venerable man became conscious of something singular in the appearance of his pastor. He seemed not fully to partake of the prevailing wonder, till Mr. Hooper had ascended the stairs, and showed himself in the pulpit, face to face with his congregation, except for the black veil. That mysterious emblem was never once withdrawn. It shook with his measured breath as he gave out the psalm; it threw its obscurity between him and the holy page, as he read the Scriptures; and while he prayed, the veil lay heavily on his uplifted countenance. Did he seek to hide it from the dread Being whom he was addressing?

Such was the effect of this simple piece of crape, that more than one woman of delicate nerves was forced to leave the meetinghouse. Yet perhaps the pale-faced congregation was almost as fearful a sight to the minister, as his black veil to them.

Mr. Hooper had the reputation of a good preacher, but not an energetic one: he strove to win his people heavenward, by mild persuasive influences, rather than to drive them thither, by the thunders of the Word. The sermon which he now delivered, was marked by the same characteristics of style and manner, as the general series of his pulpit oratory. But there was something, either in the sentiment of the discourse itself or in the imagination of the auditors, which made it greatly the most powerful effort that they had ever heard from their pastor's lips. It was tinged, rather more darkly than usual, with the gentle gloom of Mr. Hooper's temperament. The subject had reference to secret sin, and those sad mysteries which we hide from our nearest and dearest, and would fain conceal from our own consciousness, even forgetting that the Omniscient can detect them. A subtle power was breathed into his words. Each member of the congregation, the most innocent girl, and the man of hardened breast, felt as if the preacher had crept upon them, behind his awful veil, and discovered their hoarded iniquity of deed or thought. Many spread their clasped hands on their bosoms. There was nothing terrible in what Mr. Hooper said; at least, no violence; and yet, with every tremor of his melancholy voice, the hearers quaked. An unsought pathos came hand in hand with awe. So sensible were the audience of some unwonted attribute in their minister, that they longed for a breath of wind to blow aside the veil, almost believing that a stranger's visage would be discovered, though the form, gesture, and voice were those of Mr. Hooper.

At the close of the services, the people hurried out with indecorous confusion, eager to communicate their pent-up amazement, and conscious of lighter spirits, the moment they lost sight of the black veil. Some gathered in little circles, huddled closely together, with their mouths all whispering in the center; some went homeward alone, wrapt in silent meditation; some talked loudly, and profaned the Sabbath day with ostentatious laughter. A few shook their sagacious heads, intimating that they could penetrate the mystery; while one or two affirmed that there was no mystery at all, but only that Mr. Hooper's eyes were so weakened by the midnight lamp, as to require a shade. After a brief interval, forth came good Mr. Hooper also, in the rear of his flock. Turning his veiled face from one group to another, he paid due reverence to the hoary heads, saluted the middle aged with kind dignity, as their friend and spiritual guide, greeted the young with mingled authority and love, and laid his hands on the little children's heads to bless them. Such was always his custom on the Sabbath day. Strange and bewildered looks repaid him for his courtesy. None, as on former occasions, aspired to the honor of walking by their pastor's side. Old Squire Saunders, doubtless by an accidental lapse of memory, neglected to invite Mr. Hooper to his table, where the good clergyman had been wont to bless the food, almost every Sunday since his settlement. He returned, therefore, to the parsonage, and, at the moment of closing the door, was observed to look back upon the people, all of whom had their eyes fixed upon the minister. A sad smile gleamed faintly from beneath the black veil, and flickered about his mouth, glimmering as he disappeared.

"How strange," said a lady, "that a simple black veil, such as any woman might wear on her bonnet, should become such a terrible thing on Mr. Hooper's face!"

"Something must surely be amiss with Mr. Hooper's intellects," observed her husband, the physician of the village. "But the strangest part of the affair is the effect of this vagary, even on a sober-minded man like myself. The black veil, though it covers only our pastor's face, throws its influence over his whole person, and makes him ghostlike from head to foot. Do you not feel it so?"

"Truly do I," replied the lady; "and I would not be alone with him for the world. I wonder he is not afraid to be alone with himself!"

"Men sometimes are so," said her husband.

The afternoon service was attended with similar circumstances. At its conclusion, the bell tolled for the funeral of a young lady. The relatives and friends were assembled in the house, and the more distant acquaintances stood about the door, speaking of the good qualities of the deceased, when their talk was interrupted by the appearance of Mr. Hooper, still covered with his black veil. It was now an appropriate emblem. The clergyman stepped into the room where the corpse was laid, and bent over the coffin, to take a last farewell of his deceased parishioner. As he stooped, the veil hung straight down from his forehead, so that, if her eyelids had not been closed forever, the dead maiden might have seen his face. Could Mr. Hooper be fearful of her glance, that he so hastily caught back the black veil? A person, who watched the interview between the dead and the living, scrupled not to affirm, that, at the instant when the clergyman's features were disclosed, the corpse had slightly shuddered, rustling the shroud and muslin cap, though the countenance retained the composure of death. A superstitious old woman was the only witness of this prodigy. From the coffin, Mr. Hooper passed into the chamber of the mourners, and thence to the head of the staircase, to make the funeral prayer. It was a tender and heart-dissolving prayer, full of sorrow, yet so imbued with celestial hopes, that the music of a heavenly harp, swept by the fingers of the dead, seemed faintly to be heard among the accents of the minister. The people trembled, though they but darkly understood him, when he prayed that they, and himself, and all of mortal race, might be ready, as he trusted this young maiden had been, for the dreadful hour that should snatch the veil from their faces. The bearers went heavily forth, and the mourners followed, saddening all the street, with the dead before them, and Mr. Hooper in his black veil behind.

"Why do you look back?" said one in the procession to his partner.

"I had a fancy," replied she, "that the minister and the maiden's spirit were walking hand in hand."

"And so had I, at the same moment," said the other.

That night, the handsomest couple in Milford village were to be joined in wedlock. Though reckoned a melancholy man, Mr. Hooper had a placid cheerfulness for such occasions, which often excited a sympathetic smile, where livelier merriment would have been thrown away. There was no quality of his disposition which made him more beloved than this. The company at the wedding awaited his arrival with impatience, trusting that the strange awe, which had gathered over him throughout the day, would now be dispelled. But such was not the result. When Mr. Hooper came, the first thing that their eyes rested on was the same horrible black veil, which had added deeper gloom to the funeral, and could portend nothing but evil to the wedding. Such was its immediate effect on the guests, that a cloud seemed to have rolled duskily from beneath the black crape, and dimmed the light of the candles. The bridal pair stood up before the minister. But the bride's cold fingers quivered in the tremulous hand of the bridegroom, and her deathlike paleness caused a whisper, that the maiden who had been buried a few hours before, was come from her grave to be married. If ever another wedding were so dismal, it was that famous one, where they tolled the wedding knell. After performing the ceremony, Mr. Hooper raised a glass of wine to his lips, wishing happiness to the new-married couple, in a strain of mild pleasantry that ought to have brightened the features of the guests, like a cheerful gleam from the hearth. At that instant, catching a glimpse of his figure in the looking glass, the black veil involved his own spirit in the horror with which it overwhelmed all others. His frame shuddered—his lips grew white—he spilt the untasted wine upon the carpet—and rushed forth into the darkness. For the Earth, too, had on her Black Veil.

The next day, the whole village of Milford talked of little else than Parson Hooper's black veil. That, and the mystery concealed behind it, supplied a topic for discussion between acquaintances meeting in the street, and good women gossiping at their open windows. It was the first item of news that the tavern keeper told to his guests. The children babbled of it on their way to school. One imitative little imp covered his face with an old black handkerchief, thereby so affrighting his playmates, that the panic seized himself, and he well nigh lost his wits by his own waggery.

It was remarkable, that, of all the busybodies and impertinent people in the parish, not one ventured to put the plain question to Mr. Hooper, wherefore he did this thing. Hitherto, whenever there appeared the slightest call for such interference, he had never lacked advisers, nor shown himself averse to be guided by their judgment. If he erred at all, it was by so painful a degree of self-distrust, that even the mildest censure would lead him to consider an indifferent action as a crime. Yet, though so well acquainted with this amiable weakness, no individual among his parishioners chose to make the black veil a subject of friendly remonstrance. There was a feeling of dread, neither plainly confessed nor carefully concealed, which caused each to shift the responsibility upon another, till at length it was found expedient to send a deputation of the church, in order to deal with Mr. Hooper about the mystery, before it should grow into a scandal. Never did an embassy so ill discharge its duties. The minister received them with friendly courtesy, but became silent, after they were seated, leaving to his visitors the whole burthen of introducing their important business. The topic, it might be supposed, was obvious enough. There was the black veil, swathed around Mr. Hooper's forehead, and concealing every feature above his placid mouth, on which, at times, they could perceive the glimmering of a melancholy smile. But that piece of crape, to their imagination, seemed to hang down before his heart, the symbol of a fearful secret between him and them. Were the veil but cast aside, they might speak freely of it, but not till then. Thus they sat a considerable time, speechless, confused, and shrinking uneasily from Mr. Hooper's eye, which they felt to be fixed upon them with an invisible glance. Finally, the deputies returned abashed to their constituents, pronouncing the matter too weighty to be handled, except by a council of the churches, if, indeed, it might not require a general synod.

But there was one person in the village, unappalled by the awe with which the black veil had impressed all besides herself. When the deputies returned without an explanation, or even venturing to demand one, she, with the calm energy of her character, determined to chase away the strange cloud that appeared to be settling around Mr. Hooper, every moment more darkly than before. As his plighted wife, it should be her privilege to know what the black veil concealed. At the minister's first visit, therefore, she entered upon the subject, with a direct simplicity, which made the task easier both for him and her. After he had seated himself, she fixed her eyes steadfastly upon the veil, but could discern nothing of the dreadful gloom that had so overawed the multitude: it was but a double fold of crape, hanging down from his forehead to his mouth, and slightly stirring with his breath.

"No," said she aloud, and smiling, "there is nothing terrible in this piece of crape, except that it hides a face which I am always glad to look upon. Come, good sir, let the sun shine from behind the cloud. First lay aside your black veil: then tell me why you put it on."

Mr. Hooper's smile glimmered faintly.

"There is an hour to come," said he, "when all of us shall cast aside our veils. Take it not amiss, beloved friend, if I wear this piece of crape till then."

"Your words are a mystery too," returned the young lady. "Take away the veil from them, at least."

"Elizabeth, I will," said he, "so far as my vow may suffer me. Know, then, this veil is a type and a symbol, and I am bound to wear it ever, both in light and darkness, in solitude before the gaze of multitudes, and as with strangers, so with my familiar friends. No mortal eye will see it withdrawn. This dismal shade must separate me from the world: even you, Elizabeth, can never come behind it!"

"What grievous affliction hath befallen you," she earnestly inquired, "that you should thus darken your eyes forever?"

"If it be a sign of mourning," replied Mr. Hooper, "I, perhaps, like most other mortals, have sorrows dark enough be typified by a black veil."

"But what if the world will not believe that it is the type of an innocent sorrow?" urged Elizabeth. "Beloved and respected as you are, there may be whispers, that you hide your face under the consciousness of secret sin. For the sake of your holy office, do away this scandal!"

The color rose into her cheeks, as she intimated the nature of the rumors that were already abroad in the village. But Mr. Hooper's mildness did not forsake him. He even smiled again—that same sad smile, which always appeared like a faint glimmering of light, proceeding from the obscurity beneath the veil.

"If I hide my face for sorrow, there is cause enough," he merely replied. "and if I cover it for secret sin, what mortal might not do the same?"

And with this gentle, but unconquerable obstinacy, did he resist all her entreaties. At length Elizabeth sat silent. For a few moments she appeared lost in thought, considering, probably, what new methods might be tried, to withdraw her lover from so dark a fantasy, which, if it had no other meaning, was perhaps a symptom of mental disease. Though of a firmer character than his own, the tears rolled down her cheeks. But, in an instant, as it were, a new feeling took the place of sorrow: her eyes were fixed insensibly on the black veil, when, like a sudden twilight in the air, its terrors fell around her. She arose, and stood trembling before him.

"And do you feel it then at last?" said he mournfully.

She made no reply, but covered her eyes with her hand, and turned to leave the room. He rushed forward and caught her arm.

"Have patience with me, Elizabeth!" cried he passionately. "Do not desert me, though this veil must be between us here on earth. Be mine, and hereafter there shall be no veil over my face, no darkness between our souls! It is but a mortal veil—it is not for eternity! Oh! You know not how lonely I am, and how frightened to be alone behind my black veil. Do not leave me in this miserable obscurity forever!"

"Lift the veil but once, and look me in the face," said she.

"Never! It cannot be!" replied Mr. Hooper.

"Then, farewell!" said Elizabeth.

She withdrew her arm from his grasp, and slowly departed, pausing at the door, to give one long, shuddering gaze, that seemed almost to penetrate the mystery of the black veil. But, even amid his grief, Mr. Hooper smiled to think that only a material emblem had separated him from happiness, though the horrors which it shadowed forth, must be drawn darkly between the fondest of lovers.

From that time no attempts were made to remove Mr. Hooper's black veil, or, by a direct appeal, to discover the secret which it was supposed to hide. By persons who claimed a superiority to popular prejudice, it was reckoned merely an eccentric whim, such as often mingles with the sober actions of men otherwise rational, and tinges them all with its own semblance of insanity. But with the multitude, good Mr. Hooper was irreparably a bugbear. He could not walk the streets with any peace of mind, so conscious was he that the gentle and timid would turn aside to avoid him, and that others would make it a point of hardihood to throw themselves in his way. The impertinence of the latter class compelled him to give up his customary walk, at sunset, to the burial ground, for when he leaned pensively over the gate, there would always be faces behind the gravestones, peeping at his black veil. A fable went the rounds, that the stare of the dead people drove him thence. It grieved him, to the very depth of his kind heart, to observe how the children fled from his approach, breaking up their merriest sports, while his melancholy figure was yet afar off. Their instinctive dread caused him to feel, more strongly than aught else, that a preternatural horror was interwoven with the threads of the black crape. In truth, his own antipathy to the veil was known to be so great, that he never willingly passed before a mirror, nor stooped to drink at a still fountain, lest, in its peaceful bosom, he should be affrighted by himself. This was what gave plausibility to the whispers, that Mr. Hooper's conscience tortured him for some great crime, too horrible to be entirely concealed, or otherwise than so obscurely intimated. Thus, from beneath the black veil, there rolled a cloud into the sunshine, an ambiguity of sin or sorrow, which enveloped the poor minister, so that love or sympathy could never reach him. It was said, that ghost and fiend consorted with him there. With self-shudderings and outward terrors, he walked continually in its shadow, groping darkly within his own soul, or gazing through a medium that saddened the whole world. Even the lawless wind, it was believed, respected his dreadful secret, and never blew aside the veil. But still good Mr. Hooper sadly smiled, at the pale visages of the worldly throng as he passed by.

Among all its bad influences, the black veil had the one desirable effect, of making its wearer a very efficient clergyman. By the aid of his mysterious emblem—for there was no other apparent cause—he became a man of awful power, over souls that were in agony for sin. His converts always regarded him with a dread peculiar to themselves, affirming, though but figuratively, that, before he brought them to celestial light, they had been with him behind the black veil. Its gloom, indeed, enabled him to sympathize with all dark affections. Dying sinners cried aloud for Mr. Hooper, and would not yield their breath till he appeared; though ever, as he stooped to whisper consolation, they shuddered at the veiled face so near their own. Such were the terrors of the black veil, even when Death had bared his visage! Strangers came long distances to attend service at his church, with the mere idle purpose of gazing at his figure, because it was forbidden them to behold his face. But many were made to quake ere they departed! Once, during Governor Belcher's administration, Mr. Hooper was appointed to preach the election sermon. Covered with his black veil, he stood before the chief magistrate, the council, and the representatives, and wrought so deep an impression, that the legislative measures of that year, were characterized by all the gloom and piety of our earliest ancestral sway.

In this manner Mr. Hooper spent a long life, irreproachable in outward act, yet shrouded in dismal suspicions; kind and loving, though unloved, and dimly feared; a man apart from men, shunned in their health and joy, but ever summoned to their aid in mortal anguish. As years wore on, shedding their snows above his sable veil, he acquired a name throughout the New England churches, and they called him Father Hooper. Nearly all his parishioners, who were of mature age when he was settled, had been borne away by many a funeral: he had one congregation in the church, and a more crowded one in the churchyard; and having wrought so late into the evening, and done his work so well, it was now good Father Hooper's turn to rest.

Several persons were visible by the shaded candlelight, in the death chamber of the old clergyman. Natural connections he had none. But there was the decorously grave, though unmoved physician, seeking only to mitigate the last pangs of the patient whom he could not save. There were the deacons, and other eminently pious members of his church. There, also, was the Reverend Mr. Clark, of Westbury, a young and zealous divine, who had ridden in haste to pray by the bedside of the expiring minister. There was the nurse, no hired handmaiden of death, but one whose calm affection had endured thus long, in secrecy, in solitude, amid the chill of age, and would not perish, even at the dying hour. Who, but Elizabeth! And there lay the hoary head of good Father Hooper upon the death pillow, with the black veil still swathed about his brow and reaching down over his face, so that each more difficult gasp of his faint breath caused it to stir. All through life that piece of crape had hung between him and the world: it had separated him from cheerful brotherhood and woman's love, and kept him in that saddest of all prisons, his own heart; and still it lay upon his face, as if to deepen the gloom of his darksome chamber, and shade him from the sunshine of eternity.

For some time previous, his mind had been confused, wavering doubtfully between the past and the present, and hovering forward, as it were, at intervals, into the indistinctness of the world to come. There had been feverish turns, which tossed him from side to side, and wore away what little strength he had. But in his most convulsive struggles, and in the wildest vagaries of his intellect, when no other thought retained its sober influence, he still showed an awful solicitude lest the black veil should slip aside. Even if his bewildered soul could have forgotten, there was a faithful woman at his pillow, who, with averted eyes, would have covered that aged face, which she had last beheld in the comeliness of manhood. At length the death-stricken old man lay quietly in the torpor of mental and bodily exhaustion, with an imperceptible pulse, and breath that grew fainter and fainter, except when a long, deep, and irregular inspiration seemed to prelude the flight of his spirit.

The minister of Westbury approached the bedside.

"Venerable Father Hooper," said he, "the moment of your release is at hand. Are you ready for the lifting of the veil that shuts in time from eternity?"

Father Hooper at first replied merely by a feeble motion of his head; then, apprehensive, perhaps, that his meaning might be doubtful, he exerted himself to speak.

"Yea," said he, in faint accents, "my soul hath a patient weariness until that veil be lifted."

"And is it fitting," resumed the Reverend Mr. Clark, "that a man so given to prayer, of such a blameless example, holy in deed and thought, so far as mortal judgment may pronounce; is it fitting that a father in the church should leave a shadow on his memory, that may seem to blacken a life so pure? I pray you, my venerable brother, let not this thing be! Suffer us to be gladdened by your triumphant aspect, as you go to your reward. Before the veil of eternity be lifted, let me cast aside this black veil from your face!"

And thus speaking, the Reverend Mr. Clark bent forward to reveal the mystery of so many years. But, exerting a sudden energy, that made all the beholders stand aghast, Father Hooper snatched both his hands from beneath the bedclothes, and pressed them strongly on the black veil, resolute to struggle, if the minister of Westbury would contend with a dying man.

"Never!" cried the veiled clergyman. "On earth, never!"

"Dark old man!" exclaimed the affrighted minister, "with what horrible crime upon your soul are you now passing to the judgment?"

Father Hooper's breath heaved; it rattled in his throat; but, with a mighty effort, grasping forward with his hands, he caught hold of life, and held it back till he should speak. He even raised himself in bed; and there he sat, shivering with the arms of death around him, while the black veil hung down, awful, at that last moment, in the gathered terrors of a lifetime. And yet the faint, sad smile, so often there, now seemed to glimmer from its obscurity, and linger on Father Hooper's lips.

"Why do you tremble at me alone?" cried he, turning his veiled face around the circle of pale spectators. "Tremble also at each other! Have men avoided me, and women shown no pity, and children screamed and fled, only for my black veil? What, but the mystery which it obscurely typifies, has made this piece of crape so awful? When the friend shows his inmost heart to his friend; the lover to his best beloved; when man does not vainly shrink from the eye of his Creator, loathsomely treasuring up the secret of his sin; then deem me a monster, for the symbol beneath which I have lived, and die! I look around me, and, lo! On every visage a Black Veil!"

While his auditors shrank from one another, in mutual affright, Father Hooper fell back upon his pillow, a veiled corpse, with a faint smile lingering on the lips. Still veiled, they laid him in his coffin, and a veiled corpse they bore him to the grave. The grass of many years has sprung up and withered on that grave, the burial stone is moss-grown, and good Mr. Hooper's face is dust; but awful is still the thought, that it moldered beneath the Black Veil!

Why does the Black Veil horrify everyone who sees it?

1. Why does the congregation respond with "one accord" to Hooper's appearance? (19)

2. What does the old woman mean when she says that "he has changed himself into something awful, only by hiding his face"? (20)

3. Why is "more than one woman of delicate nerves" forced to leave the meetinghouse because of the minister's veil? (21)

4. During Hooper's sermon, why do all of the people in the meetinghouse feel that he has "discovered their hoarded iniquity of deed or thought"? (21)

5. Why are people's reactions so varied when they leave the meetinghouse after Hooper's first sermon with the veil?

6. Why does the whole village, including the children, talk about the veil?

7. Why can't the delegates of the church, who are sent to talk to Hooper about the veil, even mention it to him?

8. Why is Elizabeth the only person who can talk to Hooper about the veil?

Why does Hooper refuse to remove the veil?

1. Why doesn't Hooper react to his parishoners' astonishment on the first day he wears the veil?

2. Why will no one walk with Hooper or invite him home after the sermon?

3. Why does Hooper vow to wear the veil for the rest of his life?

4. Why does Hooper tell Elizabeth about his vow only when she directly questions him? What does he mean when he says that "this veil is a type and a symbol"? (25)

5. Why, although he begs Elizabeth to stay, does Hooper refuse to remove the veil even when she tells him she will stay if he will take it off?

6. Why won't Hooper let the Reverend Mr. Clark, the minister who visits him at his deathbed, lift the veil?

7. Why is Hooper buried still wearing the veil? Why is the thought "awful" that his face "moldered beneath the Black Veil!"? (30)

Why are Hooper's last words "I look around me, and, lo! On every visage a Black Veil!"?

1. Why does Hooper give a sermon on secret sin the day he first wears the veil?

2. Does the story indicate that Hooper has sinned?

3. When Hooper sees himself in the mirror at the wedding, why is he overwhelmed with horror?

4. When Elizabeth says that others may think the veil a symbol of secret sin, why does Hooper say that "if I hide my face for sorrow, there is cause enough . . . and if I cover it for secret sin, what mortal might not do the same?" (26)

5. Why does the veil keep Hooper "in that saddest of all prisons, his own heart"? (29)

6. When he is dying, why won't Hooper answer the Reverend Mr. Clark's direct question, "with what horrible crime upon your soul are you now passing to the judgment?" (30)

7. Why does Hooper tell those gathered around his deathbed to shudder at each other as well as at him?

Ethan Brand

A Chapter from an Abortive Romance

Nathaniel Hawthorne

Bartram, the lime burner, a rough, heavy-looking man, begrimed with charcoal, sat watching his kiln, at nightfall, while his little son played at building houses with the scattered fragments of marble; when, on the hillside below them, they heard a roar of laughter, not mirthful, but slow, and even solemn, like a wind shaking the boughs of the forest.

"Father, what is that?" asked the little boy, leaving his play, and pressing betwixt his father's knees.

"Oh, some drunken man, I suppose," answered the lime burner;—"some merry fellow from the barroom in the village, who dared not laugh loud enough within doors, lest he should blow the roof of the house off. So here he is, shaking his jolly sides, at the foot of Graylock."

"But, father," said the child, more sensitive than the obtuse, middle-aged clown, "he does not laugh like a man that is glad. So the noise frightens me!"

"Don't be a fool, child!" cried his father, gruffly. "You will never make a man, I do believe; there is too much of your mother in you. I have known the rustling of a leaf startle you. Hark! Here comes the merry fellow now. You shall see that there is no harm in him."

Bartram and his little son, while they were talking thus, sat watching the same limekiln that had been the scene of Ethan Brand's solitary and meditative life, before he began his search for the Unpardonable Sin. Many years, as we have seen, had now elapsed, since that portentous night when the IDEA was first developed. The kiln, however, on the mountainside, stood unimpaired, and was in nothing changed, since he had thrown his dark thoughts into the intense glow of its furnace, and melted them, as it were, into the one thought that took possession of his life. It was a rude, round, towerlike structure, about twenty feet high, heavily built of rough stones, and with a hillock of earth heaped about the larger part of its circumference; so that blocks and fragments of marble might be drawn by cartloads, and thrown in at the top. There was an opening at the bottom of the tower, like an oven mouth, but large enough to admit a man in a stooping posture, and provided with a massive iron door. With the smoke and jets of flame issuing from the chinks and crevices of this door, which seemed to give admittance into the hillside, it resembled nothing so much as the private entrance to the infernal regions, which the shepherds of the Delectable Mountains were accustomed to show to pilgrims.

There are many such limekilns in that tract of country, for the purpose of burning the white marble which composes a large part of the substance of the hills. Some of them, built years ago, and long deserted, with weeds growing in the vacant round of the interior, which is open to the sky, and grass and wild-flowers rooting themselves into the chinks of the stones, look already like relics of antiquity, and may yet be overspread with the lichens of centuries to come. Others, where the lime burner still feeds his daily and nightlong fire, afford points of interest to the wanderer among the hills, who seats himself on a log of wood or a fragment of marble, to hold chat with the solitary man. It is a lonesome, and, when the character is inclined to thought, may be an intensely thoughtful occupation; as it proved in the case of Ethan Brand, who had mused to such strange purpose, in days gone by, while the fire in this very kiln was burning.

The man who now watched the fire was of a different order, and troubled himself with no thoughts save the very few that were requisite to his business. At frequent intervals he flung back the clashing weight of the iron door, and, turning his face from the insufferable glare, thrust in huge logs of oak, or stirred the immense brands with a long pole. Within the furnace was seen the curling and riotous flames, and the burning marble, almost molten with the intensity of heat; while, without, the reflection of the fire quivered on the dark intricacy of the surrounding forest, and showed, in the foreground, a bright and ruddy little picture of the hut, the spring beside its door, the athletic and coal-begrimed figure of the lime burner, and the half-frightened child, shrinking into the protection of his father's shadow. And when, again, the iron door was closed, then reappeared the tender light of the half-full moon, which vainly strove to trace out the indistinct shapes of the neighboring mountains; and, in the upper sky, there was a flitting congregation of clouds, still faintly tinged with the rosy sunset, though, thus far down into the valley, the sunshine had vanished long and long ago.

The little boy now crept still closer to his father, as footsteps were heard ascending the hillside, and a human form thrust aside the bushes that clustered beneath the trees.

"Halloo! Who is it?" cried the lime burner, vexed at his son's timidity, yet half-infected by it. "Come forward, and show yourself, like a man; or I'll fling this chunk of marble at your head!"

"You offer me a rough welcome," said a gloomy voice, as the unknown man drew nigh. "Yet I neither claim nor desire a kinder one, even at my own fireside."

To obtain a distincter view, Bartram threw open the iron door of the kiln, whence immediately issued a gush of fierce light, that smote full upon the stranger's face and figure. To a careless eye, there appeared nothing very remarkable in his aspect, which was that of a man in a coarse, brown, country-made suit of clothes, tall and thin, with the staff and heavy shoes of a wayfarer. As he advanced, he fixed his eyes, which were very bright, intently upon the brightness of the furnace, as if he beheld, or expected to behold, some object worthy of note within it.

"Good evening, stranger," said the lime burner, "whence come you, so late in the day?"

"I come from my search," answered the wayfarer; "for, at last, it is finished."

"Drunk, or crazy!" muttered Bartram to himself. "I shall have trouble with the fellow. The sooner I drive him away, the better."

The little boy, all in a tremble, whispered to his father, and begged him to shut the door of the kiln, so that there might not be so much light; for that there was something in the man's face which he was afraid to look at, yet could not look away from. And, indeed, even the lime burner's dull and torpid sense began to be impressed by an indescribable something in that thin, rugged, thoughtful visage, with the grizzled hair hanging wildly about it, and those deeply sunken eyes, which gleamed like fires within the entrance of a mysterious cavern. But, as he closed the door, the stranger turned toward him, and spoke in a quiet, familiar way, that made Bartram feel as if he were a sane and sensible man, after all.

"Your task draws to an end, I see," said he. "This marble has already been burning three days. A few hours more will convert the stone to lime."

"Why, who are you?" exclaimed the lime burner. "You seem as well acquainted with my business as I myself."

"And well I may be," said the stranger, "for I followed the same craft, many a long year; and here, too, on this very spot. But you are a newcomer in these parts. Did you never hear of Ethan Brand?"

"The man that went in search of the Unpardonable Sin?" asked Bartram, with a laugh.

"The same," answered the stranger. "He has found what he sought, and therefore he comes back again."

"What! Then you are Ethan Brand, himself?" cried the lime burner in amazement. "I am a newcomer here, as you say; and they call it eighteen years since you left the foot of Graylock. But, I can tell you, the good folks still talk about Ethan Brand, in the village yonder, and what a strange errand took him away from his limekiln. Well, and so you have found the Unpardonable Sin?"

"Even so!" said the stranger, calmly.

"If the question is a fair one," proceeded Bartram, "where might it be?"

Ethan Brand laid his finger on his own heart. "Here!" replied he.

And then, without mirth in his countenance, but as if moved by an involuntary recognition of the infinite absurdity of seeking throughout the world for what was the closest of all things to himself, and looking into every heart, save his own, for what was hidden in no other breast, he broke into a laugh of scorn. It was the same slow, heavy laugh, that had almost appalled the lime burner, when it heralded the wayfarer's approach.

The solitary mountainside was made dismal by it. Laughter, when out of place, mistimed, or bursting forth from a disordered state of feeling, may be the most terrible modulation of the human voice. The laughter of one asleep, even if it be a little child—the madman's laugh—the wild, screaming laugh of a born idiot, are sounds that we sometimes tremble to hear, and would always willingly forget. Poets have imagined no utterance of fiends or hobgoblins so fearfully appropriate as a laugh. And even the obtuse lime burner felt his nerves shaken, as this strange man looked inward at his own heart, and burst into laughter that rolled away into the night, and was indistinctly reverberated among the hills.

"Joe," said he to his little son, "scamper down to the tavern in the village, and tell the jolly fellows there that Ethan Brand has come back, and that he has found the Unpardonable Sin!"

The boy darted away on his errand, to which Ethan Brand made no objection, nor seemed hardly to notice it. He sat on a log of wood, looking steadfastly at the iron door of the kiln. When the child was out of sight, and his swift and light footsteps ceased to be heard, treading first on the fallen leaves, and then on the rocky mountain path, the lime burner began to regret his departure. He felt that the little fellow's presence had been a barrier between his guest and himself, and that he now must deal, heart to heart, with a man who, on his own confession, had committed the only crime for which Heaven could afford no mercy. That crime, in its indistinct blackness, seemed to overshadow him. The lime burner's own sins rose up within him, and made his memory riotous with a throng of evil shapes that asserted their kindred with the Master Sin, whatever it might be, which it was within the scope of man's corrupted nature to conceive and cherish. They were all of one family; they went to and fro between his breast and Ethan Brand's, and carried dark greetings from one to the other.

Then Bartram remembered the stories which had grown traditionary in reference to this strange man, who had come upon him like a shadow of the night, and was making himself at home in his old place, after so long absence that the dead people, dead and buried for years, would have had more right to be at home, in any familiar spot, than he. Ethan Brand, it was said, had conversed with Satan himself, in the lurid blaze of this very kiln. The legend had been matter of mirth heretofore, but looked grisly now. According to this tale, before Ethan Brand departed on his search, he had been accustomed to evoke a fiend from the hot furnace of the limekiln, night after night, in order to confer with him about the Unpardonable Sin; the man and the fiend each laboring to frame the image of some mode of guilt, which could neither be atoned for, nor forgiven. And, with the first gleam of light upon the mountaintop, the fiend crept in at the iron door, there to abide in the intensest element of fire, until again summoned forth to share in the dreadful task of extending man's possible guilt beyond the scope of Heaven's else infinite mercy.

While the lime burner was struggling with the horror of these thoughts, Ethan Brand rose from the log and flung open the door of the kiln. The action was in such accordance with the idea in Bartram's mind, that he almost expected to see the Evil One issue forth, red-hot from the raging furnace.

"Hold, hold!" cried he, with a tremulous attempt to laugh; for he was ashamed of his fears, although they overmastered him. "Don't, for mercy's sake, bring out your devil now!"

"Man!" sternly replied Ethan Brand, "What need have I of the devil? I have left him behind me on my track. It is with such halfway sinners as you that he busies himself. Fear not, because I open the door. I do but act by old custom, and am going to trim your fire, like a lime burner, as I was once."

He stirred the vast coals, thrust in more wood, and bent forward to gaze into the hollow prison house of the fire, regardless of the fierce glow that reddened upon his face. The lime burner sat watching him, and half suspected his strange guest of a purpose, if not to evoke a fiend, at least to plunge bodily into the flames, and thus vanish from the sight of man. Ethan Brand, however, drew quietly back, and closed the door of the kiln.

"I have looked," said he, "into many a human heart that was seven times hotter with sinful passions than yonder furnace is with fire. But I found not there what I sought. No; not the Unpardonable Sin!"

"What is the Unpardonable Sin?" asked the lime burner, and then he shrank farther from his companion, trembling lest his question should be answered.

"It is a sin that grew within my own breast," replied Ethan Brand, standing erect, with the pride that distinguishes all enthusiasts of his stamp. "A sin that grew nowhere else! The sin of an intellect that triumphed over the sense of brotherhood with man, and reverence for God, and sacrificed everything to its own mighty claims! The only sin that deserves a recompense of immortal agony! Freely, were it to do again, would I incur the guilt. Unshrinkingly, I accept the retribution!"

"The man's head is turned," muttered the lime burner to himself. "He may be a sinner, like the rest of us—nothing more likely—but I'll be sworn, he is a madman, too."

Nevertheless, he felt uncomfortable at his situation, alone with Ethan Brand on the wild mountainside, and was right glad to hear the rough murmur of tongues, and the footsteps of what seemed a pretty numerous party, stumbling over the stones, and rustling through the underbrush. Soon appeared the whole lazy regiment that was wont to infest the village tavern, comprehending three or four individuals who had drunk flip beside the barroom fire, through all the winters, and smoked their pipes beneath the stoop, through all the summers since Ethan Brand's departure. Laughing boisterously, and mingling all their voices together in unceremonious talk, they now burst into the moonshine and narrow streaks of firelight that illuminated the open space before the limekiln. Bartram set the door ajar again, flooding the spot with light, that the whole company might get a fair view of Ethan Brand, and he of them.

There, among other old acquaintances, was a once ubiquitous man, now almost extinct, but whom we were formerly sure to encounter at the hotel of every thriving village throughout the country. It was the stage-agent. The present specimen of the genus was a wilted and smoke-dried man, wrinkled and red-nosed, in a smartly cut, brown, bobtailed coat, with brass buttons, who, for a length of time unknown, had kept his desk and corner in the barroom, and was still puffing what seemed to be the same cigar that he had lighted twenty years before. He had great fame as a dry joker, though, perhaps, less on account of any intrinsic humor, than from a certain flavor of brandy-toddy and tobacco smoke, which impregnated all his ideas and expressions, as well as his person. Another well-remembered, though strangely altered face was that of Lawyer Giles, as people still called him in courtesy; an elderly ragamuffin, in his soiled shirtsleeves and tow-cloth trousers. This poor fellow had been an attorney, in what he called his better days, a sharp practitioner, and in great vogue among the village litigants; but flip, and sling, and toddy, and cocktails, imbibed at all hours, morning, noon, and night, had caused him to slide from intellectual, to various kinds and degrees of bodily labor, till, at last, to adopt his own phrase, he slid into a soap vat. In other words, Giles was now a soap boiler, in a small way. He had come to be but the fragment of a human being, a part of one foot having been chopped off by an ax, and an entire hand torn away by the devilish grip of a steam engine. Yet, though the corporeal hand was gone, a spiritual member remained; for, stretching forth the stump, Giles steadfastly averred, that he felt an invisible thumb and fingers, with as vivid a sensation as before the real ones were amputated. A maimed and miserable wretch he was; but one, nevertheless, whom the world could not trample on, and had no right to scorn, either in this or any previous stage of his misfortunes, since he had still kept up the courage and spirit of a man, asked nothing in charity, and, with his one hand—and that the left one—fought a stern battle against want and hostile circumstances.

Among the throng, too, came another personage, who, with certain points of similarity to Lawyer Giles, had more of difference. It was the village doctor, a man of some fifty years, whom, at an earlier period of his life, we should have introduced as paying a professional visit to Ethan Brand, during the latter's supposed insanity. He was now a purple-visaged, rude, and brutal, yet half-gentlemanly figure, something wild, ruined, and desperate in his talk, and in all the details of his gesture and manners. Brandy possessed this man like an evil spirit, and made him as surly and savage as a wild beast, and as miserable as a lost soul; but there was supposed to be in him such wonderful skill, such native gifts of healing, beyond any which medical science could impart, that society caught hold of him, and would not let him sink out of its reach. So, swaying to and fro upon his horse, and grumbling thick accents at the bedside, he visited all the sick chambers for miles about among the mountain towns; and sometimes raised a dying man, as it were, by miracle, or, quite as often, no doubt, sent his patient to a grave that was dug many a year too soon. The doctor had an everlasting pipe in his mouth, and, as somebody said, in allusion to his habit of swearing, it was always alight with hellfire.

These three worthies pressed forward, and greeted Ethan Brand, each after his own fashion, earnestly inviting him to partake of the contents of a certain black bottle; in which, as they averred, he would find something far better worth seeking for, than the Unpardonable Sin. No mind, which has wrought itself, by intense and solitary meditation, into a high state of enthusiasm, can endure the kind of contact with low and vulgar modes of thought and feeling, to which Ethan Brand was now subjected. It made him doubt—and, strange to say, it was a painful doubt—whether he had indeed found the Unpardonable Sin, and found it within himself. The whole question on which he had exhausted life, and more than life, looked like a delusion.

"Leave me," he said bitterly, "ye brute beasts, that have made yourselves so, shriveling up your souls with fiery liquors! I have done with you. Years and years ago, I groped into your hearts and found nothing there for my purpose. Get ye gone!"

"Why, you uncivil scoundrel," cried the fierce doctor, "is that the way you respond to the kindness of your best friends? Then let me tell you the truth. You have no more found the Unpardonable Sin than yonder boy Joe has. You are but a crazy fellow—I told you so, twenty years ago—neither better nor worse than a crazy fellow, and the fit companion of old Humphrey, here!"

He pointed to an old man, shabbily dressed, with long white hair, thin visage, and unsteady eyes. For some years past, this aged person had been wandering about among the hills, inquiring of all travelers whom he met, for his daughter. The girl, it seemed, had gone off with a company of circus performers; and, occasionally, tidings of her came to the village, and fine stories were told of her glittering appearance, as she rode on horseback in the ring, or performed marvelous feats on the tightrope.

The white-haired father now approached Ethan Brand, and gazed unsteadily into his face.

"They tell me you have been all over the earth," said he, wringing his hands with earnestness. "You must have seen my daughter; for she makes a grand figure in the world, and everybody goes to see her. Did she send any word to her old father, or say when she is coming back?"

Ethan Brand's eye quailed beneath the old man's. That daughter, from whom he so earnestly desired a word of greeting, was the Esther of our tale; the very girl whom, with such cold and remorseless purpose, Ethan Brand had made the subject of a psychological experiment, and wasted, absorbed, and perhaps annihilated her soul, in the process.

"Yes," murmured he, turning away from the hoary wanderer; "it is no delusion. There is an Unpardonable Sin!"

While these things were passing, a merry scene was going forward in the area of cheerful light, beside the spring and before the door of the hut. A number of the youth of the village, young men and girls, had hurried up the hillside, impelled by curiosity to see Ethan Brand, the hero of so many a legend familiar to their childhood. Finding nothing, however, very remarkable in his aspect—nothing but a sunburnt wayfarer, in plain garb and dusty shoes, who sat looking into the fire, as if he fancied pictures among the coals—these young people speedily grew tired of observing him. As it happened, there was other amusement at hand. An old German Jew, traveling with a diorama on his back, was passing down the mountain road toward the village, just as the party turned aside from it; and, in hopes of eking out the profits of the day, the showman had kept them company to the limekiln.

"Come, old Dutchman," cried one of the young men, "let us see your pictures, if you can swear they are worth looking at!"

"Oh, yes, Captain," answered the Jew—whether as a matter of courtesy or craft, he styled everybody Captain—"I shall show you, indeed, some very superb pictures!"

So, placing his box in a proper position, he invited the young men and girls to look through the glass orifices of the machine, and proceeded to exhibit a series of the most outrageous scratchings and daubings, as specimens of the fine arts, that ever an itinerant showman had the face to impose upon his circle of spectators. The pictures were worn out, moreover, tattered, full of cracks and wrinkles, dingy with tobacco smoke, and otherwise in a most pitiable condition.

Some purported to be cities, public edifices, and ruined castles in Europe; others represented Napoleon's battles, and Nelson's sea fights; and in the midst of these would be seen a gigantic, brown, hairy hand—which might have been mistaken for the Hand of Destiny, though, in truth, it was only the showman's—pointing its forefinger to various scenes of the conflict, while its owner gave historical illustrations. When, with much merriment at its abominable deficiency of merit, the exhibition was concluded, the German bade little Joe put his head into the box. Viewed through the magnifying glasses, the boy's round, rosy visage assumed the strangest imaginable aspect of an immense, Titanic child, the mouth grinning broadly, and the eyes, and every other feature, overflowing with fun at the joke. Suddenly, however, that merry face turned pale, and its expression changed to horror; for this easily impressed and excitable child had become sensible that the eye of Ethan Brand was fixed upon him through the glass.

"You make the little man to be afraid, Captain," said the German Jew, turning up the dark and strong outline of his visage, from his stooping posture. "But, look again; and, by chance, I shall cause you to see somewhat that is very fine, upon my word!"

Ethan Brand gazed into the box for an instant, and then starting back, looked fixedly at the German. What had he seen? Nothing, apparently; for a curious youth, who had peeped in, almost at the same moment, beheld only a vacant space of canvas.

"I remember you now," muttered Ethan Brand to the showman.

"Ah, Captain," whispered the Jew of Nuremberg, with a dark smile, "I find it to be a heavy matter in my show-box—this Unpardonable Sin! By my faith, Captain, it has wearied my shoulders, this long day, to carry it over the mountain."

"Peace!" answered Ethan Brand, sternly, "Or get thee into the furnace yonder!"

The Jew's exhibition had scarcely concluded, when a great, elderly dog—who seemed to be his own master, as no person in the company laid claim to him—saw fit to render himself the object of public notice. Hitherto, he had shown himself a very quiet, well-disposed old dog, going round from one to another, and, by way of being sociable, offering his rough head to be patted by any kindly hand that would take so much trouble. But, now, all of a sudden, this grave and venerable quadruped, of his own mere notion, and without the slightest suggestion from anybody else, began to run round after his tail, which, to heighten the absurdity of the proceeding, was a great deal shorter than it should have been. Never was seen such headlong eagerness in pursuit of an object that could not possibly be attained; never was heard such a tremendous outbreak of growling, snarling, barking, and snapping—as if one end of the ridiculous brute's body were at deadly and most unforgivable enmity with the other. Faster and faster, round about went the cur; and faster and still faster fled the unapproachable brevity of his tail; and louder and fiercer grew his yells of rage and animosity; until, utterly exhausted, and as far from the goal as ever, the foolish old dog ceased his performance as suddenly as he had begun it. The next moment, he was as mild, quiet, sensible, and respectable in his deportment, as when he first scraped acquaintance with the company.

As may be supposed, the exhibition was greeted with universal laughter, clapping of hands, and shouts of encore; to which the canine performer responded by wagging all that there was to wag of his tail, but appeared totally unable to repeat his very successful effort to amuse the spectators.

Meanwhile, Ethan Brand had resumed his seat upon the log; and, moved, it might be, by a perception of some remote analogy between his own case and that of this self-pursuing cur, he broke into the awful laugh, which, more than any other token, expressed the condition of his inward being. From that moment, the merriment of the party was at an end; they stood aghast, dreading lest the inauspicious sound should be reverberated around the horizon, and that mountain would thunder it to mountain, and so the horror be prolonged upon the ears. Then, whispering one to another, that it was late—that the moon was almost down—that the August night was growing chill—they hurried homeward, leaving the lime burner and little Joe to deal as they might with their unwelcome guest. Save for these three human beings, the open space on the hillside was a solitude, set in a vast gloom of forest. Beyond that darksome verge, the firelight glimmered on the stately trunks and almost black foliage of pines, intermixed with the lighter verdure of sapling oaks, maples, and poplars, while, here and there, lay the gigantic corpses of dead trees, decaying on the leaf-strewn soil. And it seemed to little Joe—a timorous and imaginative child— that the silent forest was holding its breath, until some fearful thing should happen.

Ethan Brand thrust more wood into the fire, and closed the door of the kiln; then looking over his shoulder at the lime burner and his son, he bade, rather than advised, them to retire to rest.

"For myself I cannot sleep," said he. "I have matters that it concerns me to meditate upon. I will watch the fire, as I used to do in the old time."

"And call the devil out of the furnace to keep you company, I suppose," muttered Bartram, who had been making intimate acquaintance with the black bottle above-mentioned. "But watch, if you like, and call as many devils as you like! For my part, I shall be all the better for a snooze. Come, Joe!"

As the boy followed his father into the hut, he looked back to the wayfarer, and the tears came into his eyes; for his tender spirit had an intuition of the bleak and terrible loneliness in which this man had enveloped himself.

When they had gone, Ethan Brand sat listening to the crackling of the kindled wood, and looking at the little spurts of fire that issued through the chinks of the door. These trifles, however, once so familiar, had but the slightest hold of his attention; while deep within his mind, he was reviewing the gradual, but marvelous change, that had been wrought upon him by the search to which he had devoted himself. He remembered how the night dew had fallen upon him—how the dark forest had whispered to him—how the stars had gleamed upon him—a simple and loving man, watching his fire in the years gone by, and ever musing as it burned. He remembered with what tenderness, with what love and sympathy for mankind, and what pity for human guilt and woe, he had first begun to contemplate those ideas which afterward became the inspiration of his life; with what reverence he had then looked into the heart of man, viewing it as a temple originally divine, and however desecrated, still to be held sacred by a brother; with what awful fear he had deprecated the success of his pursuit, and prayed that the Unpardonable Sin might never be revealed to him. Then ensued that vast intellectual development, which, in its progress, disturbed the counterpoise between his mind and heart. The Idea that possessed his life had operated as a means of education; it had gone on cultivating his powers to the highest point of which they were susceptible; it had raised him from the level of an unlettered laborer, to stand on a starlit eminence, whither the philosophers of the earth, laden with the lore of universities, might vainly strive to clamber after him. So much for the intellect! But where was the heart? That indeed, had withered—had contracted—had hardened—had perished! It had ceased to partake of the universal throb. He had lost his hold of the magnetic chain of humanity. He was no longer a brother-man, opening the chambers or the dungeons of our common nature by the key of holy sympathy, which gave him a right to share in all its secrets; he was now a cold observer, looking on mankind as the subject of his experiment, and, at length, converting man and woman to be his puppets, and pulling the wires that moved them to such degrees of crime as were demanded for his study.

Thus Ethan Brand became a fiend. He began to be so from the moment that his moral nature had ceased to keep the pace of improvement with his intellect. And now, as his highest effort and inevitable development—as the bright and gorgeous flower, and rich, delicious fruit of his life's labor—he had produced the Unpardonable Sin!

"What more have I to seek? What more to achieve?" said Ethan Brand to himself. "My task is done, and well done!"

Starting from the log with a certain alacrity in his gait, and ascending the hillock of earth that was raised against the stone circumference of the limekiln, he thus reached the top of the structure. It was a space of perhaps ten feet across, from edge to edge, presenting a view of the upper surface of the immense mass of broken marble with which the kiln was heaped. All these innumerable blocks and fragments of marble were red-hot, and vividly on fire, sending up great spouts of blue flame, which quivered aloft and danced madly, as within a magic circle, and sank and rose again, with continual and multitudinous activity. As the lonely man bent forward over this terrible body of fire, the blasting heat smote up against his person with a breath that, it might be supposed, would have scorched and shriveled him up in a moment.

Ethan Brand stood erect and raised his arms on high. The blue flames played upon his face, and imparted the wild and ghastly light which alone could have suited its expression; it was that of a fiend on the verge of plunging into his gulf of intensest torment.

"Oh, Mother Earth," cried he, "who art no more my Mother, and into whose bosom this frame shall never be resolved! Oh, mankind, whose brotherhood I have cast off, and trampled thy great heart beneath my feet! Oh, stars of Heaven, that shone on me of old, as if to light me onward and upward!—farewell all, and forever! Come, deadly element of Fire—henceforth my familiar friend! Embrace me as I do thee!"

That night the sound of a fearful peal of laughter rolled heavily through the sleep of the lime burner and his little son; the dim shapes of horror and anguish haunted their dreams, and seemed still present in the rude hovel when they opened their eyes to the daylight.

"Up, boy, up!" cried the lime burner, staring about him. "Thank Heaven, the night is gone at last; and rather than pass such another, I would watch my limekiln, wide awake, for a twelvemonth. This Ethan Brand, with his humbug of an Unpardonable Sin, has done me no such mighty favor in taking my place!"

He issued from the hut, followed by little Joe, who kept fast hold of his father's hand. The early sunshine was already pouring its gold upon the mountaintops, and though the valleys were still in shadow, they smiled cheerfully in the promise of the bright day that was hastening onward. The village, completely shut in by hills, which swelled away gently about it, looked as if it had rested peacefully in the hollow of the great hand of Providence. Every dwelling was distinctly visible; the little spires of the two churches pointed upward, and caught a fore-glimmering of brightness from the sun-gilt skies upon their gilded weathercocks. The tavern was astir, and the figure of the old, smoke-dried stage-agent, cigar in mouth, was seen beneath the stoop. Old Graylock was glorified with a golden cloud upon his head. Scattered, likewise, over the breasts of the surrounding mountains, there were heaps of hoary mist, in fantastic shapes, some of them far down into the valley, others high up toward the summits, and still others, of the same family of mist or cloud, hovering in the gold radiance of the upper atmosphere. Stepping from one to another of the clouds that rested on the hills, and thence to the loftier brotherhood that sailed in air, it seemed almost as if mortal man might thus ascend into the heavenly regions. Earth was so mingled with sky that it was a daydream to look at it.

To supply that charm of the familiar and homely, which Nature so readily adopts into a scene like this, the stagecoach was rattling down the mountain road, and the driver sounded his horn; while Echo caught up the notes and intertwined them into a rich, and varied, and elaborate harmony, of which the original performer could lay claim to little share. The great hills played a concert among themselves, each contributing a strain of airy sweetness.

Little Joe's face brightened at once.

"Dear father," cried he, skipping cheerily to and fro, "that strange man is gone, and the sky and the mountains all seem glad of it!"

"Yes," growled the lime burner with an oath, "but he has let the fire go down, and no thanks to him, if five hundred bushels of lime are not spoilt. If I catch the fellow hereabouts again I shall feel like tossing him into the furnace!"

With his long pole in his hand he ascended to the top of the kiln. After a moment's pause he called to his son.

"Come up here, Joe!" said he.

So little Joe ran up the hillock and stood by his father's side. The marble was all burnt into perfect, snow-white lime. But on its surface, in the midst of the circle—snow-white too, and thoroughly converted into lime—lay a human skeleton, in the attitude of a person who, after long toil, lies down to long repose. Within the ribs—strange to say—was the shape of a human heart.

"Was the fellow's heart made of marble?" cried Bartram, in some perplexity at this phenomenon. "At any rate, it is burnt into what looks like special good lime; and, taking all the bones together, my kiln is half a bushel the richer for him."

So saying, the rude lime burner lifted his pole, and letting it fall upon the skeleton, the relics of Ethan Brand were crumbled into fragments.

How does Ethan Brand feel about having found the Unpardonable Sin?

1. During their first encounter, why does Brand say that Bartram's welcome is "rough," but add that "I neither claim nor desire a kinder one"? (37)

2. Why does Brand give "a laugh of scorn" when he points to his own heart as the location of the Unpardonable Sin? (38)

3. What does Brand mean when he describes the Unpardonable Sin as "the sin of an intellect that triumphed over the sense of brotherhood with man, and reverence for God"? (40)

4. When the drunken crowd confronts him, why does Brand begin to doubt whether he has found the Unpardonable Sin?

5. While he is pursuing the Unpardonable Sin, why does Brand also pray that it "might never be revealed to him"? (46)

6. What does Brand see when he looks into the traveling Jew's show-box? Why does the curious youth who looks into the box see nothing?

7. Why does the narrator describe Brand's sin as the "rich, delicious fruit of his life's labor"? (47)

8. Why does Brand appeal to Mother Earth, mankind, and the stars before entering the kiln? Why does he ask Fire to "embrace me as I do thee!"? (47)

Is Ethan Brand more frightening or pathetic?

1. Why does Brand's laugh disturb those who hear it?

2. Why does Brand tell Bartram the story of finding the Unpardonable Sin?

3. What does Brand mean when he says that he left the devil "behind me on my track"? (40)

4. Why does Brand give his "awful laugh" when he sees a possible connection between himself and the old dog chasing its tail? (45)

5. Why are we told that Brand was once "simple and loving" and looked with "reverence . . . into the heart of man"? (46)

6. Why does Brand lose "his hold of the magnetic chain of humanity"? What holds this "chain" together as if it were magnetic? (46)

7. Why is Brand's heart the only part of him, besides his skeleton, that doesn't burn away? Why does it turn into "what looks like special good lime"? (49)

8. Why does the story end with Bartram crumbling Brand's skeleton into fragments?

What, if anything, does Bartram learn from his encounter with Ethan Brand?

1. Why is Bartram irritated by his son's fear of Brand?

2. Why does Bartram's son immediately fear Brand's appearance, and Bartram come to "be impressed" by an "indescribable something" in Brand's face? (37)

3. Why does Bartram send his son to the tavern to announce Brand's arrival?

4. Why, when he is alone with Brand, does Bartram think of his own sins?

5. Why are Brand's and Bartram's sins described as "all of one family"? Why does Bartram see sins going "to and fro between his breast and Ethan Brand's"? (39)

6. Why does Bartram ask what the Unpardonable Sin is, but then tremble "lest his question should be answered"? (40)

7. Why does Bartram repeatedly think that Brand is a "madman"? (40)

8. Why are Bartram's final words in the story that "taking all the bones together, my kiln is half a bushel the richer for" Ethan Brand? (49)

The Scarlet Letter

Interpretive Questions for Discussion

ઇર્જાજી

The following questions suggest a wide range of possibilities for interpretation.
Some of the questions are keyed to the passages for close reading
(pp. 69–105), and careful reading of these passages either before or during
the discussion allows you to consider the various possible answers
to the discussion questions more thoroughly.

Keep in mind that everyone, including the discussion leader, is an
equal partner in interpretation and understanding. Do not expect a teacher
or leader to provide answers to the questions that follow;
instead, listen to individual ideas during discussion, test the validity
of your own thoughts, and learn from the group.

Questions have been organized for discussion of the novel as a whole or by chapter.

What does the scarlet letter represent?

1. Why is the word *adultery* never mentioned in the novel?

Passage 3　　2. Why does Hester embroider the scarlet letter so elaborately?

3. Does the meaning of the A change in the course of the novel? If so, how? Who or what is responsible for the change or changes?

4. Does Hester's wearing of the scarlet A have the effect that the colony's leaders want it to have?

Passage 6　　5. Does Hester intend to remind people of the scarlet letter when she dresses Pearl so fantastically?

6. Why does Hester keep wearing the A even after she could remove it?

Passage 16　　7. Why does the narrator give us many interpretations of the final scene and what, if anything, is seen on Dimmesdale's bare chest? Why are we left to choose an interpretation?

8. Why does Hester and Dimmesdale's gravestone bear "the semblance of an engraved escutcheon"? How does its heraldic inscription "serve for a motto and brief description of our now concluded legend"?

How does Hawthorne intend us to assess the guilt of Hester, Dimmesdale, and Chillingworth?

1. Are we meant to agree, when Hester is contrasted with the Virgin Mary, that "the world was only the darker for this woman's beauty, and the more lost for the infant that she had borne"?

2. When Dimmesdale publicly exhorts Hester to name her child's father, does he really want her to?

Passage 4　　3. Did Chillingworth ever love Hester? Why did he marry her?

4. Why does Dimmesdale "confess" to his congregation even though he knows they will misinterpret what he says? Why does he remain a hypocrite, though a "subtle, but remorseful" one?

5. Is it pride or humility that causes Hester to hold herself apart from others? Why does she spend so much time nursing others and taking care of the poor?

6. Does Chillingworth realize he has been doing a "devil's office"? If so, could he stop himself?

7. Is Hester right to blame herself for Chillingworth's having become a "fiend"?

8. Does Hawthorne want us to think that Dimmesdale's public confession makes up for his many years of silence?

Why does the novel end with a description of the red A on the black background of Hester and Dimmesdale's tombstone?

1. Why is Hester's A scarlet?

2. How do Pearl and Chillingworth represent the dichotomy of red and black?

3. How are the colors red and black juxtaposed when Dimmesdale, Hester, and Pearl stand together on the scaffold? What meanings are associated with these colors?

4. Why is the A often associated with light?

5. Why does Hawthorne tell us that the "curious investigator" can still "perplex himself with the purport" of the tombstone?

6. Why does Hawthorne give us the "herald's wording" of the device on the tombstone? Why is there an escutcheon on the tombstone, when this symbol is usually associated with nobility?

7. In what way does the novel's final phrase echo its opening and "serve for a motto and brief description of our now concluded legend"?

8. What does it mean that the tale's somberness is "relieved only by one ever-glowing point of light gloomier than the shadow"?

The Custom House—Introductory

1. Why is it important to Hawthorne to "keep the inmost Me behind its veil" in his writing?

2. Why does Hawthorne imagine his reader as "a friend, a kind and apprehensive, though not the closest friend"?

Passage 1   3. What is Hawthorne's attitude toward the community of Salem?

Passage 1   4. Why does Hawthorne compare himself to his ancestors and take their shame on himself?

5. Of all the men who work at the Custom House, Hawthorne chooses to describe the Inspector, the General, and the man of business. What qualities do these men share? What distinguishes them from the other men?

6. What do the descriptions in "The Custom House" suggest about Hawthorne's attitude toward authority and government in the United States?

Passage 2   7. Why does Hawthorne tell his readers that *The Scarlet Letter* is based on an actual piece of cloth and a historical manuscript he found while working at the Custom House?

8. According to Hawthorne, how is the work of a "romance-writer" different from the work of other writers? Why did he find it so difficult to write a romance?

9. Why does Hawthorne repeatedly compare losing his job to having his head cut off?

Chapter 1: The Prison-Door

1. Why does the narrator describe the prison and prison door in such detail?

2. Why does the narrator tell us that a new colony must "invariably" build a prison, "whatever Utopia of human virtue and happiness they might originally project"?

3. Why are we told that the rosebush might have survived as part of the "stern old wilderness" or might have "sprung up under the footsteps of the sainted Anne Hutchinson"? How would its meaning be different in each case?

4. What power does the narrator recognize in the "deep heart of Nature"?

5. Why does the narrator present a rose to the reader and hope that it may symbolize "some sweet moral blossom" connected with the tale?

Chapter 2: The Market-Place

1. What does the narrator mean by saying that "religion and law were almost identical" for the Puritan colonists?

2. Why do the "goodwives" in the marketplace want to be responsible for Hester's punishment?

3. Why are some of the Puritan women offended when Hester emerges from the prison? *Passage 3*

4. Why does the scarlet letter have on Hester "the effect of a spell, taking her out of the ordinary relations with humanity, and enclosing her in a sphere by herself"? *Passage 3*

5. While standing on the scaffold, why does Hester see scenes from her own past rather than her actual surroundings?

6. When Hester comes back to seeing the marketplace, why does she feel that "these were her realities,—all else had vanished"?

Chapter 3: The Recognition

1. What is the "powerful emotion" that darkens the stranger's face when he looks at Hester?

2. What does the stranger mean when he says that Hester will be a "living sermon against sin"?

3. Why does the stranger insist that the father of Hester's baby "will be known"?

4. What does Governor Bellingham mean when he tells Dimmesdale that "the responsibility of this woman's [Hester's] soul lies greatly with you"?

5. Why does Hester refuse to reveal the name of her child's father?

Chapter 4: The Interview

1. Why does Chillingworth take care of the baby before talking to Hester?

2. Why does Chillingworth want Hester to live with the scarlet letter, rather than escape it through death?

Passage 4

3. Are we meant to agree with Chillingworth when he tells Hester, "Between thee and me, the scale hangs fairly balanced"?

4. Why does Hester agree to keep Chillingworth's true identity a secret?

5. Why does Hester ask Chillingworth if he is "like the Black Man that haunts the forest round about us"?

Chapter 5: Hester at Her Needle

Passage 5

1. Why does Hester choose to stay in the community and bear her punishment?

2. Why does Hester, with the approval of the magistrates, choose to live in the small thatched cottage on the outskirts of town?

3. Why does Hester's sewing become an eagerly sought after "fashion"?

4. Are we meant to agree with Hester when she thinks that the scarlet letter gives her "a sympathetic knowledge of the hidden sin in other hearts"?

5. What kind of power do the townspeople attribute to the scarlet letter? Why?

Chapter 6: Pearl

1. Why does Hester worry about Pearl's changeability and willfulness?   *Passage 6*

2. What is the significance of the name Hester gives her child?   *Passage 6*

3. Why does Pearl avoid the Puritan children and get angry if they approach her?

4. What is it that Hester sees when a "freakish, elfish cast" comes into Pearl's eyes?

5. Why does Pearl say, "I have no Heavenly Father"? Why does Hester reprimand her daughter when she says this?

Chapter 7: The Governor's Hall

1. What does the narrator think of the townspeople's plans to take Pearl away from Hester?

2. Why does Hester dress Pearl in such gorgeous, fantastic clothes?

3. Why does Pearl have a "look of naughty merriment" when she tells Hester to look at herself in the convex mirror?

4. Why does Pearl cry so furiously when Hester won't give her a red rose?

Chapter 8: The Elf-Child and the Minister

1. Why won't Pearl give the appropriate answer to the catechism question the governor asks her, even though she knows it?

2. Why does Chillingworth look uglier and more misshapen to Hester now?

3. Why is Pearl less "wild and flighty" in the presence of Dimmesdale?

4. Why does Mistress Hibbins invite Hester to the forest and tell her that she has "promised the Black Man that comely Hester Prynne should make one"?

5. Why does Hester tell Mistress Hibbins that if Pearl had been taken away from her she would have gone to the forest and signed the Black Man's book with her blood?

Chapter 9: The Leech

1. What is the significance of Prynne's choosing Chillingworth as his new name?

2. Why does the narrator tell us that many doctors of that time had "lost the spiritual view of existence"?

3. Why does Chillingworth seek out Dimmesdale as his "spiritual guide"?

4. Why does Dimmesdale put his hand over his heart whenever he is alarmed?

5. Why does Dimmesdale initially refuse Chillingworth's help?

6. If the townspeople believe that Chillingworth is "Satan's emissary," why don't they act to save Dimmesdale?

Chapter 10: The Leech and His Patient

1. Why does the narrator tell us that Chillingworth had always been "a pure and upright man"?

2. What makes Chillingworth's investigation, which began as a quest "only of truth," turn into something more sinister?

3. Why does Pearl place burrs on Hester's scarlet letter? Why doesn't Hester remove the burrs?

4. When Pearl claims that the Black Man (Chillingworth) cannot catch her, are we intended to see her as wise or naive?

5. Does Dimmesdale believe he is right to refuse Chillingworth's urging to confess?

6. Does Dimmesdale realize that Chillingworth's presence contributes to his own sickness? If so, why does Dimmesdale allow Chillingworth to continue to counsel him?

7. After looking at the sleeping Dimmesdale's breast, why does Chillingworth feel "wonder, joy, and horror" simultaneously?

Chapter 11: The Interior of a Heart

1. How, exactly, does Chillingworth make Dimmesdale suffer?

2. Could Chillingworth stop torturing Dimmesdale? How much control does Chillingworth have over his actions?

3. Why does Dimmesdale become more holy in the eyes of his congregants? Why do Dimmesdale's congregants refuse to believe him when he tells them that he is a sinner?

4. Why does Dimmesdale laugh when he whips himself?

5. Why won't Dimmesdale confess despite his suffering?

Chapter 12: The Minister's Vigil

1. Why does Dimmesdale want to stand on the scaffold with Hester and Pearl at night?

2. When describing the characters on the scaffold, the narrator refers to "little Pearl, herself a symbol." What does Pearl symbolize?

3. Why does Dimmesdale go home with Chillingworth, the man he hates?

4. Why do Dimmesdale's sermons become more powerful as he gets sicker?

5. What is the significance of the red A that Dimmesdale sees in the sky? Why are we told that others interpret it to mean "Angel"?

Chapter 13: Another View of Hester

1. Why does Hester never battle with the public, but rather submit, "uncomplainingly, to its worst usage"?

2. Why does Hester spend so much time caring for the poor and the sick? How does her work affect the meaning of the A?

3. What does it mean that Hester is no longer a "woman"?   *Passage 8*

4. Why would Puritan society have held Hester's "freedom of speculation . . . to be a deadlier crime than that stigmatized by the scarlet letter"?

5. What does Hester think must be "essentially modified" about men before women "can be allowed to assume what seems a fair and suitable position"?

6. In whose view had the scarlet letter "not done its office"? What "office" was intended, and what did the scarlet letter actually do?

Chapter 14: Hester and the Physician

1. What about Chillingworth's desire to find his wife's lover makes it "a devil's office"?

2. Are we meant to feel sympathy for Chillingworth when he describes himself as "a mortal man, with once a human heart"?

3. When Chillingworth's "moral aspect is faithfully revealed to his mind's eye," what does he see?

4. When Hester asks if the minister has suffered enough, why does Chillingworth say that Dimmesdale "has but increased the debt"?

5. Why can Chillingworth pity Hester, but not Dimmesdale?

6. Are we meant to believe Chillingworth when he says that since the moment Hester "didst plant the germ of evil . . . it has all been a dark necessity"?

Chapter 15: Hester and Pearl

1. According to the novel, is Hester correct when she says that Chillingworth "has done me worse wrong than I did him"?

2. Why is Pearl grieved to have hurt a sea bird, but apparently unmoved by the pain she causes other people?

3. Is Pearl being truthful when she tells her mother that she has "told all" she knows about the letter A and Dimmesdale's putting his hand over his heart?

4. How is Pearl a symbol of "justice and retribution" as well as "mercy and beneficence"?

5. Why doesn't Hester tell Pearl what the scarlet letter means? Why is Hester "false to the symbol on her bosom" for the first time in seven years?

Chapter 16: A Forest Walk

1. Why do Hester and Dimmesdale "need the whole wide world to breathe in" when they talk together?

2. Why does Hawthorne set the meeting between Hester and Dimmesdale in the "mystery of the primeval forest"? *Passage 11*

3. What does the narrator mean when he says that Hester had been traveling in a "moral wilderness"? *Passage 11*

4. Why does the narrator describe the forest as both a place of natural beauty and the home of the Black Man? *Passage 11*

Chapter 17: The Pastor and His Parishioner

1. When Hester and Dimmesdale first see each other, why do they each ask if the other is still alive?

2. Once they touch, why do Hester and Dimmesdale move together with "neither he nor she assuming the guidance, but with an unexpressed consent"?

3. Whose judgment of Dimmesdale's life are we meant to agree with, Dimmesdale's or Hester's?

4. According to the novel, how much responsibility does Hester bear for Dimmesdale's suffering?

5. When Hester reveals Chillingworth's real identity, why does Dimmesdale first blame Hester harshly and then forgive her?

6. Are we meant to agree with Dimmesdale when he says that "that old man's revenge has been blacker than my sin"?

7. Why does Hester suggest leaving Boston, and why does Dimmesdale agree to the plan?

Chapter 18: A Flood of Sunshine

1. When the narrator says that Hester has learned "much amiss," what is he referring to?

2. Does the narrator have more sympathy for Hester's position or for Dimmesdale's?

Passage 12   3. To what extent does removing the scarlet letter allow Hester to "undo it all, and make it as it had never been"? Why does the narrator describe the discarded symbol as "glittering like a lost jewel"?

Passage 12   4. Why is this chapter titled "A Flood of Sunshine"?

Passage 12   5. Why does Hester say that Pearl will love Dimmesdale?

Chapter 19: The Child at the Brook-Side

1. What does it mean that "Pearl was the oneness of Hester and Dimmesdale's being"?

2. Why does Pearl refuse to come to Hester until she puts the scarlet letter back on?

3. Why does Hawthorne repeatedly use the brook to reflect Pearl's image?

4. Why does Pearl answer her mother's order to bring the scarlet letter to her with "Come thou and take it up!"?

5. Why does Pearl kiss the scarlet letter and refuse to embrace Dimmesdale?

Chapter 20: The Minister in a Maze

1. What is the significance of Hester and Dimmesdale's decision to return to the Old World?

2. Why does Dimmesdale have so much more physical energy on his return from the forest?

3. Why does Dimmesdale feel that if he does the wicked things he is tempted to do "it would be at once involuntary and intentional"? How could Dimmesdale's actions be both "involuntary" and "intentional"?

4. Why is Dimmesdale suddenly tempted "to do some strange, wild, wicked thing" to every member of the community he encounters? Why is he tempted to contaminate others with words?

5. After burning his first Election Sermon, why does Dimmesdale write the second version so quickly?

Chapter 21: The New England Holiday

1. On Election Day, why does Hester dress just as she has for the last seven years?

2. What does it mean that Pearl "was the gem on her mother's unquiet bosom"?

3. Why does Pearl describe Dimmesdale as a "strange, sad man" and draw contrasts between the way he behaves in the day and in the darkness?

4. Why are we given such a complete portrait of the crowd assembled in the marketplace?

5. Why does Chillingworth let Hester learn from the ship's captain that the physician plans to sail with Hester and Dimmesdale to the Old World?

Chapter 22: The Procession

1. Why does the narrator so closely describe the order of the people in the procession, their names, and their appearance?

2. Why is Hester chilled by the contrast she feels between Dimmesdale in the forest and in the marketplace?

3. Why does Hester tell Pearl that "we must not always talk in the marketplace of what happens to us in the forest"?

Passage 14

4. Why are we told so much about the tone in which Dimmesdale speaks his sermon, but given none of the sermon's words?

5. Why does Hester feel that "her whole orb of life, both before and after, was connected with this spot" at the foot of the scaffold, "as with the one point that gave it unity"?

6. Why does Hawthorne have "the self-same" women appear in this marketplace scene as appeared at the novel's beginning? Why is the compassionate woman with the child the one who has died?

Chapter 23: The Revelation

1. At what point does Dimmesdale decide to confess? What makes him determine to do so?

2. Why does Hester go to Dimmesdale against her will?

3. What gives Dimmesdale the strength to resist Chillingworth's temptation? Why is Chillingworth's power "not what it was"?

4. Why does Dimmesdale ask for Hester's strength, but add "but let it be guided by the will which God hath granted me!"?

5. Why are we told that Dimmesdale "threw off all assistance" before making the final revelation of his guilt?

6. Why are we told that when Pearl kisses Dimmesdale "a spell was broken"? Why are her tears "the pledge that she would grow up amid human joy and sorrow, nor forever do battle with the world, but be a woman in it"?

7. Why does Hester plead for assurance that she and Dimmesdale will meet again after death? Why does Dimmesdale respond by telling her to hush?

Chapter 24: Conclusion

1. Why does the narrator refer to Chillingworth as an "unhumanized mortal"?

2. Why does Chillingworth leave all his property to Pearl?

3. Why does Hawthorne have Pearl end up in the Old World as an aristocrat?

4. What is "more real" about the life that Hester can lead in New England? Why does she start wearing the scarlet letter again?

5. Why does Hester start telling women that the whole relationship between men and women will change for the better?

6. Why are Hester and Dimmesdale buried side by side, but with a space in between?

The Scarlet Letter

Passages and Questions
for Close Reading

*The questions that follow these passages encourage close reading
and, taken together, constitute a rigorous study of literary themes, techniques,
and terms. All readers will benefit from the challenges these questions
pose, and students in honors courses or courses qualifying for college credit
will find these questions useful for exam preparation.*

Passage 1

But the sentiment has likewise its moral quality. The figure of that first ancestor, invested by family tradition with a dim and dusky grandeur, was present to my boyish imagination, as far back as I can remember. It still haunts me, and induces a sort of home-feeling with the past, which I scarcely claim in reference to the present phase of the town. I seem to have a stronger claim to a residence here on account of this grave, bearded, sable-cloaked, and steeple-crowned progenitor,—who came so early, with his Bible, and his sword, and trode the unworn street with such a stately port, and made so large a figure, as a man of war and peace,—a stronger claim than for myself, whose name is seldom heard and my face hardly known. He was a soldier, legislator, judge; he was a ruler in the Church; he had all the Puritanic traits, both good and evil. He was likewise a bitter persecutor as witness the Quakers, who have remembered him in their histories, and relate an incident of his hard severity towards a woman of their sect, which will last longer, it is to be feared, than any record of his better deeds, although these were many. His son, too, inherited the persecuting spirit, and made himself so conspicuous in the martyrdom of the witches, that their blood may fairly be said to have left a stain upon him. So deep a stain, indeed, that his old dry bones, in the Charter Street burial-ground, must still retain it, if they have not crumbled utterly to dust! I know not whether these ancestors of mine bethought themselves to repent, and ask pardon of Heaven for their cruelties; or whether they are now groaning under the heavy consequences of them, in another state of being. At all events, I, the present writer, as their representative, hereby take shame upon myself for their sakes, and pray that any curse incurred by them—as I have heard, and as the dreary and unprosperous condition of the race, for many a long year back, would argue to exist—may be now and henceforth removed.

1. What is the effect of Hawthorne's claiming that his ancestors were "invested by family tradition with a *dim* and *dusky* grandeur" (emphasis added)?

2. What contrast does the narrator suggest by saying that the figure of his ancestor both "haunts me" and "induces a sort of home-feeling with the past"? What do these feelings reveal about the narrator's state of mind?

3. What comparison does the narrator draw between his ancestor's presence and his own? What specific words and phrases convey this comparison?

4. What literary technique is Hawthorne employing when he says that the witches' blood has stained his ancestor so deeply that "his old dry bones, in the Charter Street burial-ground, must still retain it, if they have not crumbled utterly to dust!"? What does this technique suggest about Hawthorne's attitude toward his ancestor John Hathorne, one of the judges for the Salem witchcraft trials?

5. What is the effect of the phrase set off by dashes ("—as I have heard, and as the dreary and unprosperous condition of the race, for many a long year back, would argue to exist—") in the last sentence of this passage?

Passage 2

But the object that most drew my attention, in the mysterious package, was a certain affair of fine red cloth, much worn and faded. There were traces about it of gold embroidery, which, however, was greatly frayed and defaced; so that none, or very little, of the glitter was left. It had been wrought, as was easy to perceive, with wonderful skill of needlework; and the stitch (as I am assured by ladies conversant with such mysteries) gives evidence of a now forgotten art, not to be recovered even by the process of picking out the threads. This rag of scarlet cloth,—for time and wear and a sacrilegious moth, had reduced it to little other than a rag,—on careful examination, assumed the shape of a letter. It was the capital letter A. By an accurate measurement, each limb proved to be precisely three inches and a quarter in length. It had been intended, there could be no doubt, as an ornamental article of dress; but how it was to be worn, or what rank, honor, and dignity, in by-past times, were signified by it, was a riddle which (so evanescent are the fashions of the world in these particulars) I saw little hope of solving. And yet it strangely interested me. My eyes fastened themselves upon the old scarlet letter, and would not be turned aside. Certainly, there was some deep meaning in it, most worthy of interpretation, and which, as it were, streamed forth from the mystic symbol, subtly communicating itself to my sensibilities, but evading the analysis of my mind.

While thus perplexed,—and cogitating, among other hypotheses, whether the letter might not have been one of those decorations which the white men used to contrive, in order to take the eyes of Indians,—I happened to place it on my breast. It seemed to me,—the reader may smile, but must not doubt my word,—it seemed to me, then, that I experienced a sensation not altogether physical, yet almost so, as of burning heat; and as if the letter were not of red cloth, but red-hot iron. I shuddered, and involuntarily let it fall upon the floor.

1. What adjectives does the narrator use to describe the scarlet letter? What is the cumulative effect of his description of it?

2. Why does Hawthorne describe the stitching on the fabric as a "forgotten art"? What effect does he create by saying that the stitching could not be discovered "even by the process of picking out the threads"?

3. How does Hawthorne convey the hold that the scarlet letter exerts on the narrator's imagination? What does this suggest about the letter's power as a symbol?

4. What is the effect of the narrator's saying "the reader may smile, but must not doubt my word"? What relationship with the reader is implied here?

5. What is the effect of the qualifications that the narrator makes about how the letter feels when he puts it on ("a sensation not altogether physical, yet almost so . . . as if the letter were not of red cloth")?

Passage 3

The door of the jail being flung open from within, there appeared, in the first place, like a black shadow emerging into the sunshine, the grim and grisly presence of the town-beadle, with a sword by his side and his staff of office in his hand. This personage prefigured and represented in his aspect the whole dismal severity of the Puritanic code of law, which it was his business to administer in its final and closest application to the offender. Stretching forth the official staff in his left hand, he laid his right upon the shoulder of a young woman, whom he thus drew forward; until, on the threshold of the prison-door, she repelled him, by an action marked with natural dignity and force of character, and stepped into the open air, as if by her own free will. She bore in her arms a child, a baby of some three months old, who winked and turned aside its little face from the too vivid light of day; because its existence, heretofore, had brought it acquainted only with the gray twilight of a dungeon, or other darksome apartment of the prison.

When the young woman—the mother of this child—stood fully revealed before the crowd, it seemed to be her first impulse to clasp the infant closely to her bosom; not so much by an impulse of motherly affection, as that she might thereby conceal a certain token, which was wrought or fastened into her dress. In a moment, however, wisely judging that one token of her shame would but poorly serve to hide another, she took the baby on her arm, and, with a burning blush, and yet a haughty smile, and a glance that would not be abashed, looked around at her townspeople and neighbors. On the breast of her gown, in fine red cloth, surrounded with an elaborate embroidery and fantastic flourishes of gold-thread, appeared the letter A. It was so artistically done, and with so much fertility and gorgeous luxuriance of fancy, that it had all the effect of a last and fitting decoration to the apparel which she wore; and which was of a splendor in accordance with the taste of the age, but greatly beyond what was allowed by the sumptuary regulations of the colony.

The young woman was tall, with a figure of perfect elegance on a large scale. She had dark and abundant hair, so glossy that it threw off the sunshine with a gleam, and a face which, besides being beautiful from regularity of feature and richness of complexion, had the impressiveness belonging to a marked brow and deep black eyes. She was lady-like, too, after the manner of the feminine gentility of those days; characterized by a certain state and dignity, rather than by the delicate, evanescent, and indescribable grace, which is now recognized as its indication. And never had Hester Prynne appeared more lady-like, in the antique interpretation of the term, than as she issued from the prison. Those who had before known her, and had expected to behold her dimmed and obscured by a disastrous cloud, were astonished, and even startled, to perceive how her beauty shone out, and made a halo of the misfortune and ignominy in which she was enveloped. It may be true, that, to a sensitive observer, there was something exquisitely painful in it. Her attire, which, indeed, she had wrought for the occasion, in prison, and had modelled much after her own fancy, seemed to express the attitude of her spirit, the desperate recklessness of her mood, by its wild and picturesque peculiarity. But the point which drew all eyes, and, as it were, transfigured the wearer,—so that both men and women, who had been familiarly acquainted with Hester Prynne, were now impressed as if they beheld her for the first time,—was that SCARLET LETTER, so fantastically embroidered and illuminated upon her bosom. It had the effect of a spell, taking her out of the ordinary relations with humanity, and enclosing her in a sphere by herself.

1. What literary technique is Hawthorne using when he says that the town-beadle "prefigured and represented in his aspect the whole dismal severity of the Puritanic code of law"? What about the town-beadle's "aspect" represents the "Puritanic code of law"?

2. What is the effect of Hester's reacting to the crowd's scrutiny with both "a burning blush" and a "haughty smile"? What does this add to her characterization?

3. What adjectives and adverbs does the narrator use to describe the scarlet letter? What do these suggest about Hester's character and her reaction to her punishment?

4. What technique is Hawthorne using when he writes that "her beauty shone out, and made a halo of the misfortune and ignominy in which she was enveloped"? What does this add to our understanding of the relationship between Hester and the crowd?

Passage 4

"Hester," said he, "I ask not wherefore, nor how, thou hast fallen into the pit, or say, rather, thou hast ascended to the pedestal of infamy, on which I found thee. The reason is not far to seek. It was my folly, and thy weakness. I,—a man of thought,—the bookworm of great libraries,—a man already in decay, having given my best years to feed the hungry dream of knowledge,—what had I to do with youth and beauty like thine own! Misshapen from my birth-hour, how could I delude myself with the idea that intellectual gifts might veil physical deformity in a young girl's fantasy! Men call me wise. If sages were ever wise in their own behoof, I might have foreseen all this. I might have known that, as I came out of the vast and dismal forest, and entered this settlement of Christian men, the very first object to meet my eyes would be thyself, Hester Prynne, standing up, a statue of ignominy, before the people. Nay, from the moment when we came down the old church steps together, a married pair, I might have beheld the bale-fire of that scarlet letter blazing at the end of our path!"

"Thou knowest," said Hester,—for, depressed as she was, she could not endure this last quiet stab at the token of her shame,—"thou knowest that I was frank with thee. I felt no love, nor feigned any."

"True!" replied he. "It was my folly! I have said it. But, up to that epoch of my life, I had lived in vain. The world had been so cheerless! My heart was a habitation large enough for many guests, but lonely and chill, and without a household fire. I longed to kindle one! It seemed not so wild a dream,—old as I was, and sombre as I was, and misshapen as I was,—that the simple bliss, which is scattered far and wide, for all mankind to gather up, might yet be mine. And so, Hester, I drew thee into my heart, into its innermost chamber, and sought to warm thee by the warmth which thy presence made there!"

"I have greatly wronged thee," murmured Hester.

"We have wronged each other," answered he. "Mine was the first wrong, when I betrayed thy budding youth into a false and unnatural relation with my decay. Therefore, as a man who has not thought and philosophized in vain, I seek no vengeance, plot no evil against thee. Between thee and me, the scale hangs fairly balanced. But, Hester, the man lives who has wronged us both! Who is he?"

"Ask me not!" replied Hester Prynne, looking firmly into his face. "That thou shalt never know!"

"Never, sayest thou?" rejoined he, with a smile of dark and self-relying intelligence. "Never know him! Believe me, Hester, there are few things,—whether in the outward world, or, to a certain depth, in the invisible sphere of thought,—few things hidden from the man who devotes himself earnestly and unreservedly to the solution of a mystery. Thou mayest cover up thy secret from the prying multitude. Thou mayest conceal it, too, from the ministers and magistrates, even as thou didst this day, when they sought to wrench the name out of thy heart, and give thee a partner on thy pedestal. But, as for me, I come to the inquest with other senses than they possess. I shall seek this man, as I have sought truth in books; as I have sought gold in alchemy. There is a sympathy that will make me conscious of him. I shall see him tremble. I shall feel myself shudder, suddenly and unawares. Sooner or later, he must needs be mine!"

1. What do Chillingworth's exclamations reveal about his past with Hester and his mental and emotional state in this interview?

2. What contrast does Chillingworth draw between other people and himself when he describes how he will discover the father of Hester's child? What does this contrast reveal about his character?

3. What is the tone of Chillingworth's speech before he asks Hester to name the man "who has wronged us both" as compared to the tone of his speech following her reply that "thou shalt never know"?

4. What is the tone of Chillingworth's statement that "he must needs be mine"? How does this line serve as the emotional climax of this scene?

Passage 5

It may seem marvellous, that, with the world before her,—kept by no restrictive clause of her condemnation within the limits of the Puritan settlement, so remote and so obscure,—free to return to her birthplace, or to any other European land, and there hide her character and identity under a new exterior, as completely as if emerging into another state of being,—and having also the passes of the dark, inscrutable forest open to her, where the wildness of her nature might assimilate itself with a people whose customs and life were alien from the law that had condemned her,—it may seem marvellous that this woman should still call that place her home, where, and where only, she must needs be the type of shame. But there is a fatality, a feeling so irresistible and inevitable that it has the force of doom, which almost invariably compels human beings to linger around and haunt, ghostlike, the spot where some great and marked event has given the color to their lifetime; and still the more irresistibly, the darker the tinge that saddens it. Her sin, her ignominy, were the roots which she had struck into the soil. It was as if a new birth, with stronger assimilations than the first, had converted the forest-land, still so uncongenial to every other pilgrim and wanderer, into Hester Prynne's wild and dreary, but life-long home. All other scenes of earth—even that village of rural England, where happy infancy and stainless maidenhood seemed yet to be in her mother's keeping, like garments put off long ago—were foreign to her, in comparison. The chain that bound her here was of iron links, and galling to her inmost soul, but never could be broken.

It might be, too,—doubtless it was so, although she hid the secret from herself, and grew pale whenever it struggled out of her heart, like a serpent from its hole,—it might be that another feeling kept her within the scene and pathway that had been so fatal. There dwelt, there trode the feet of one with whom she deemed herself connected in a union, that, unrecognized on earth, would bring them together before the bar of final judgment, and make that their marriage-altar, for a joint futurity of endless retribution. Over and over again, the tempter of souls had thrust this idea upon Hester's contemplation, and laughed at the passionate and desperate joy with which she seized, and then strove to cast it from her. She barely looked the idea in the face, and hastened to bar it in its dungeon. What she compelled herself to believe,—what, finally, she reasoned upon, as her motive for continuing a resident of New England,—was half a truth, and half a self-delusion. Here, she said to herself, had been the scene of her guilt, and here should be the scene of her earthly punishment; and so, perchance, the torture of her daily shame would at length purge her soul, and work out another purity than that which she had lost; more saint-like, because the result of martyrdom.

Hester Prynne, therefore, did not flee.

1. What is the effect of Hawthorne's including so many dependent clauses in the sentence that begins "It may seem marvellous"? What sense does this sentence give us of Hester's decision to stay in Boston?

2. Why does the narrator describe the forest as "dark" and "inscrutable"?

3. What words in the sentence that begins "But there is a fatality" convey pain and gloom? What does this sentence add to our sense of what Hester's decision means?

4. What literary technique is Hawthorne using when he writes that Hester's "sin, her ignominy, were the roots which she had struck into the soil"? What does this comparison add to the overall effect of the passage?

5. What technique is Hawthorne using when he writes that Hester "barely looked the idea in the face, and hastened to bar it in its dungeon"? How does this technique contribute to our sense of Hester's mental state?

Passage 6

We have as yet hardly spoken of the infant; that little creature, whose innocent life had sprung, by the inscrutable decree of Providence, a lovely and immortal flower, out of the rank luxuriance of a guilty passion. How strange it seemed to the sad woman, as she watched the growth, and the beauty that became every day more brilliant, and the intelligence that threw its quivering sunshine over the tiny features of this child! Her Pearl!—For so had Hester called her; not as a name expressive of her aspect, which had nothing of the calm, white, unimpassioned lustre that would be indicated by the comparison. But she named the infant "Pearl," as being of great price,—purchased with all she had,—her mother's only treasure! How strange, indeed! Man had marked this woman's sin by a scarlet letter, which had such potent and disastrous efficacy that no human sympathy could reach her, save it were sinful like herself. God, as a direct consequence of the sin which man thus punished, had given her a lovely child, whose place was on that same dishonored bosom, to connect her parent for ever with the race and descent of mortals, and to be finally a blessed soul in heaven! Yet these thoughts affected Hester Prynne less with hope than apprehension. She knew that her deed had been evil; she could have no faith, therefore, that its result would be for good. Day after day, she looked fearfully into the child's expanding nature, ever dreading to detect some dark and wild peculiarity, that should correspond with the guiltiness to which she owed her being.

Certainly, there was no physical defect. By its perfect shape, its vigor, and its natural dexterity in the use of all its untried limbs, the infant was worthy to have been brought forth in Eden; worthy to have been left there, to be the plaything of the angels, after the world's first parents were driven out. The child had a native grace which does not invariably coexist with faultless beauty, its attire, however simple, always impressed the beholder as if it were the very garb that precisely became it best. But little Pearl was not clad in rustic weeds. Her mother, with a morbid purpose, that may be better understood hereafter, had bought the richest tissues that could be procured, and allowed her imaginative faculty its full play in the arrangement and decoration of the dresses which the child wore, before the public eye. So magnificent was the small figure, when thus arrayed, and such was the splendor of Pearl's own proper beauty, shining through the gorgeous robes which might have extinguished a paler loveliness, that there was an absolute circle of radiance around her, on the darksome cottage floor. And yet a russet gown, torn and soiled with the child's rude play, made a picture of her just as perfect. Pearl's aspect was imbued with a spell of infinite variety; in this one child there were many children, comprehending the full scope between the wild-flower prettiness of a peasant-baby, and the pomp, in little, of an infant princess. Throughout all, however, there was a trait of passion, a certain depth of hue, which she never lost; and if, in any of her changes, she had grown fainter or paler, she would have ceased to be herself,— it would have been no longer Pearl!

This outward mutability indicated, and did not more than fairly express, the various properties of her inner life. Her nature appeared to possess depth, too, as well as variety; but—or else Hester's fears deceived her—it lacked reference and adaptation to the world into which she was born. The child could not be made amenable to rules. In giving her existence, a great law had been broken; and the result was a being whose elements were perhaps beautiful and brilliant, but all in disorder; or with an order peculiar to themselves, amidst which the point of variety and arrangement was difficult or impossible to be discovered. Hester could only account for the child's character—and even then most vaguely and imperfectly—by recalling what she herself had been, during that momentous period while Pearl was imbibing her soul from the spiritual world, and her bodily frame from its material of earth. The mother's impassioned state had been the medium through which were transmitted to the unborn infant the rays of its moral life; and, however white and clear originally, they had taken the deep stains of crimson and gold, the fiery lustre, the black shadow, and the untempered light of the intervening substance. Above all, the warfare of Hester's spirit, at that epoch, was perpetuated in Pearl. She could recognize her wild, desperate, defiant mood, the flightiness of her temper, and even some of the very cloud-shapes of gloom and despondency that had brooded in her heart. They were now illuminated by the morning radiance of a young child's disposition, but later in the day of earthly existence might be prolific of the storm and whirlwind.

1. What technique is Hawthorne using when he describes Pearl as "a lovely and immortal flower" which has sprung "out of the rank luxuriance of a guilty passion"? What does this contrast suggest about Pearl's nature and Hester's guilt?

2. What symbolic meanings does Hawthorne associate with Pearl's name?

3. What comparisons and contrasts does this passage draw between Pearl and the scarlet letter? What do these add to our sense of Hester's spiritual situation?

4. In the sentence beginning "The mother's impassioned state," what emotional effects are symbolized or produced by the colors crimson, gold, and black?

5. What kind of metaphor is Hawthorne developing in the last two sentences of this passage? What does this comparison reveal about Pearl's nature?

Passage 7

Walking in the shadow of a dream, as it were, and perhaps actually under the influence of a species of somnambulism, Mr. Dimmesdale reached the spot where, now so long since, Hester Prynne had lived through her first hours of public ignominy. The same platform or scaffold, black and weather-stained with the storm or sunshine of seven long years, and footworn, too, with the tread of many culprits who had since ascended it, remained standing beneath the balcony of the meeting-house. The minister went up the steps.

It was an obscure night of early May. An unvaried pall of cloud muffled the whole expanse of sky from zenith to horizon. If the same multitude which had stood as eyewitnesses while Hester Prynne sustained her punishment could now have been summoned forth, they would have discerned no face above the platform, nor hardly the outline of a human shape, in the dark gray of the midnight. But the town was all asleep. There was no peril of discovery. The minister might stand there, if it so pleased him, until morning should redden in the east, without other risk than that the dank and chill night-air would creep into his frame, and stiffen his joints with rheumatism, and clog his throat with catarrh and cough; thereby defrauding the expectant audience of to-morrow's prayer and sermon. No eye could see him, save that ever-wakeful one which had seen him in his closet, wielding the bloody scourge. Why, then, had he come hither? Was it but the mockery of penitence? A mockery, indeed, but in which his soul trifled with itself! A mockery at which angels blushed and wept, while fiends rejoiced, with jeering laughter! He had been driven hither by the impulse of that Remorse which dogged him everywhere, and whose own sister and closely linked companion was that Cowardice which invariably drew him back, with her tremulous gripe, just when the other impulse had hurried him to the verge of a disclosure. Poor, miserable man! what right had infirmity like his to burden itself with crime? Crime is for the iron-nerved, who have their choice either to endure it, or, if it press too hard, to exert their fierce and savage strength for a good purpose, and fling it off at once! This feeble and most sensitive of spirits could do neither, yet continually did one thing or another, which intertwined, in the same inextricable knot, the agony of heaven-defying guilt and vain repentance.

And thus, while standing on the scaffold, in this vain show of expiation, Mr. Dimmesdale was overcome with a great horror of mind, as if the universe were gazing at a scarlet token on his naked breast, right over his heart. On that spot, in very truth, there was, and there had long been, the gnawing and poisonous tooth of bodily pain. Without any effort of his will, or power to restrain himself, he shrieked aloud; an outcry that went pealing through the night, and was beaten back from one house to another, and reverberated from the hills in the background; as if a company of devils, detecting so much misery and terror in it, had made a plaything of the sound, and were bandying it to and fro.

1. What do the references to "somnambulism" and "walking in the shadow of a dream" suggest about Dimmesdale's state of mind as he climbs the scaffold?

2. How does Hawthorne emphasize the amount of time that has passed since Hester climbed the scaffold? Why is this important for assessing what Dimmesdale is doing?

3. What specific words and phrases does Hawthorne use to convey the futility of what Dimmesdale is doing?

4. What technique is Hawthorne using when he describes the remorse and cowardice that torment Dimmesdale? How does this heighten our sense of the minister's conflicted state of mind?

Passage 8

The rulers, and the wise learned men of the community, were longer in acknowledging the influence of Hester's good qualities than the people. The prejudices which they shared in common with the latter were fortified in themselves by an iron framework of reasoning, that made it a far tougher labor to expel them. Day by day, nevertheless, their sour and rigid wrinkles were relaxing into something which, in the due course of years, might grow to be an expression of almost benevolence. Thus it was with the men of rank, on whom their eminent position imposed the guardianship of the public morals. Individuals in private life, meanwhile, had quite forgiven Hester Prynne for her frailty; nay, more, they had begun to look upon the scarlet letter as the token, not of that one sin, for which she had borne so long and dreary a penance, but of her many good deeds since. "Do you see that woman with the embroidered badge?" they would say to strangers. "It is our Hester,—the town's own Hester, who is so kind to the poor, so helpful to the sick, so comfortable to the afflicted!" Then, it is true, the propensity of human nature to tell the very worst of itself, when embodied in the person of another, would constrain them to whisper the black scandal of bygone years. It was none the less a fact, however, that, in the eyes of the very men who spoke thus, the scarlet letter had the effect of the cross on a nun's bosom. It imparted to the wearer a kind of sacredness, which enabled her to walk securely amid all peril. Had she fallen among thieves, it would have kept her safe. It was reported, and believed by many, that an Indian had drawn his arrow against the badge, and that the missile struck it, but fell harmless to the ground.

The effect of the symbol—or, rather, of the position in respect to society that was indicated by it—on the mind of Hester Prynne herself, was powerful and peculiar. All the light and graceful foliage of her character had been withered up by this red-hot brand, and had long ago fallen away, leaving a bare and harsh outline, which might have been repulsive, had she possessed friends or companions to be repelled by it. Even the attractiveness of her person had undergone a similar change. It might be partly owing to the studied austerity of her dress, and partly to the lack of demonstration in her manners. It was a sad transformation, too, that her rich and luxuriant hair had either been cut off, or was so completely hidden by a cap, that not a shining lock of it ever once gushed into the sunshine. It was due in part to all these causes, but still more to something else, that there seemed to be no longer anything in Hester's face for Love to dwell upon; nothing in Hester's form, though majestic and statue-like, that Passion would ever dream of clasping in its embrace; nothing in Hester's bosom, to make it ever again the pillow of Affection. Some attribute had departed from her, the permanence of which had been essential to keep her a woman. Such is frequently the fate, and such the stern development, of feminine character and person, when the woman has encountered, and lived through, an experience of peculiar severity. If she be all tenderness, she will die. If she survive, the tenderness will either be crushed out of her, or—and the outward semblance is the same—crushed so deeply into her heart that it can never show itself more. The latter is perhaps the truest theory. She who has once been woman, and ceased to be so, might at any moment become a woman again if there were only the magic touch to effect the transfiguration. We shall see whether Hester Prynne were ever afterwards so touched, and so transfigured.

1. What is the narrator's attitude toward the "wise and learned men of the community"? What specific words and phrases reveal this attitude?

2. What does it mean that it is "the propensity of human nature to tell the very worst of itself, when embodied in the person of another"? What is the narrator's tone here?

3. How does the narrator seem to feel about Hester's transformation? What words and phrases communicate his feeling?

4. How is being a woman defined in this passage?

5. Why does the narrator switch to the first person in the last sentence of the passage?

Passage 9

It is remarkable that persons who speculate the most boldly often conform with the most perfect quietude to the external regulations of society. The thought suffices them, without investing itself in the flesh and blood of action. So it seemed to be with Hester. Yet, had little Pearl never come to her from the spiritual world, it might have been far otherwise. Then, she might have come down to us in history, hand in hand with Anne Hutchinson, as the foundress of a religious sect. She might, in one of her phases, have been a prophetess. She might, and not improbably would, have suffered death from the stern tribunals of the period, for attempting to undermine the foundations of the Puritan establishment. But, in the education of her child, the mother's enthusiasm of thought had something to wreak itself upon. Providence, in the person of this little girl, had assigned to Hester's charge the germ and blossom of womanhood, to be cherished and developed amid a host of difficulties. Everything was against her. The world was hostile. The child's own nature had something wrong in it, which continually betokened that she had been born amiss,—the effluence of her mother's lawless passion,—and often impelled Hester to ask, in bitterness of heart, whether it were for ill or good that the poor little creature had been born at all.

Indeed, the same dark question often rose into her mind, with reference to the whole race of womanhood. Was existence worth accepting, even to the happiest among them? As concerned her own individual existence, she had long ago decided in the negative, and dismissed the point as settled. A tendency to speculation, though it may keep woman quiet, as it does man, yet makes her sad. She discerns, it may be, such a hopeless task before her. As a first step, the whole system of society is to be torn down, and built up anew. Then, the very nature of the opposite sex, or its long hereditary habit, which has become like nature, is to be essentially modified, before woman can be allowed to assume what seems a fair and suitable position. Finally, all other difficulties being obviated, woman cannot take advantage of these preliminary reforms, until she herself shall have undergone a still mightier change; in which, perhaps, the ethereal essence, wherein she has her truest life, will be found to have evaporated. A woman never overcomes these problems by any exercise of thought. They are not to be solved, or only in one way. If her heart chance to come uppermost, they vanish. Thus, Hester Prynne, whose heart had lost its regular and healthy throb, wandered without a clew in the dark labyrinth of mind; now turned aside by an insurmountable precipice; now starting back from a deep chasm. There was wild and ghastly scenery all around her, and a home and comfort nowhere. At times, a fearful doubt strove to possess her soul, whether it were not better to send Pearl at once to heaven, and go herself to such futurity as Eternal Justice should provide.

The scarlet letter had not done its office.

1. Does the narrator seem to admire or criticize Hester's nature when he says that she might have been "the foundress of a religious sect" or a "prophetess"?

2. What is "the very nature of the opposite sex, or its long hereditary habit, which has become like nature" that must be modified before women can "assume what seems a fair and suitable position"? Does the narrator seem to be in favor of this modification?

3. What is woman's "ethereal essence, wherein she has her truest life" which may "be found to have evaporated" if women seek to take a different place in society?

4. When the narrator says that these problems "vanish" if a woman's "heart chance to come uppermost," what is he implying about the women's arguments for changes in society?

5. If, as the narrator implies, Hester conforms to the "external regulations of society," why has the scarlet letter "not done its office"?

Passage 10

Her final employment was to gather sea-weed, of various kinds, and make herself a scarf, or mantle, and a head-dress, and thus assume the aspect of a little mermaid. She inherited her mother's gift for devising drapery and costume. As the last touch to her mermaid's garb, Pearl took some eel-grass, and imitated, as best she could, on her own bosom, the decoration with which she was so familiar on her mother's. A letter,—the letter A,—but freshly green, instead of scarlet! The child bent her chin upon her breast, and contemplated this device with strange interest; even as if the one only thing for which she had been sent into the world was to make out its hidden import.

"I wonder if mother will ask me what it means!" thought Pearl.

Just then, she heard her mother's voice, and flitting along as lightly as one of the little sea-birds, appeared before Hester Prynne, dancing, laughing, and pointing her finger to the ornament upon her bosom.

"My little Pearl," said Hester, after a moment's silence, "the green letter, and on thy childish bosom, has no purport. But dost thou know, my child, what this letter means which thy mother is doomed to wear?"

"Yes, mother," said the child. "It is the great letter A. Thou hast taught me in the horn-book."

Hester looked steadily into her little face; but, though there was that singular expression which she had so often remarked in her black eyes, she could not satisfy herself whether Pearl really attached any meaning to the symbol. She felt a morbid desire to ascertain the point.

"Dost thou know, child, wherefore thy mother wears this letter?"

"Truly do I!" answered Pearl, looking brightly into her mother's face. "It is for the same reason that the minister keeps his hand over his heart!"

"And what reason is that?" asked Hester, half smiling at the absurd incongruity of the child's observation; but, on second thoughts, turning pale. "What has the letter to do with any heart, save mine?"

"Nay, mother, I have told all I know," said Pearl, more seriously than she was wont to speak. "Ask yonder old man whom thou hast been talking with! It may be he can tell. But in good earnest now, mother dear, what does this scarlet letter mean?—and why dost thou wear it on thy bosom? —and why does the minister keep his hand over his heart?"

1. What does it mean that Pearl's A is "freshly green, instead of scarlet"? What does this suggest about Pearl's nature?

2. Is Pearl being malicious when she wonders if Hester will ask her what the A means? What details of the passage lead you to your answer?

3. What does the conversation between Hester and Pearl reveal about their relationship? How do the narrator's asides contribute to the sense of their relationship?

4. Why is it described as an "absurd incongruity" when Pearl connects Hester's scarlet letter to Dimmesdale's holding his hand over his heart?

5. What is the effect of Pearl's asking three linked questions ("what does this scarlet letter mean?—and why dost thou wear it on thy bosom?—and why does the minister keep his hand over his heart?")? Why does she ask these questions "more seriously than she was wont to speak"?

Passage 11

The road, after the two wayfarers had crossed from the peninsula to the mainland, was no other than a footpath. It straggled onward into the mystery of the primeval forest. This hemmed it in so narrowly, and stood so black and dense on either side, and disclosed such imperfect glimpses of the sky above, that, to Hester's mind, it imaged not amiss the moral wilderness in which she had so long been wandering. The day was chill and sombre. Overhead was a gray expanse of cloud, slightly stirred, however, by a breeze; so that a gleam of flickering sunshine might now and then be seen at its solitary play along the path. This flitting cheerfulness was always at the farther extremity of some long vista through the forest. The sportive sunlight—feebly sportive, at best, in the predominant pensiveness of the day and scene—withdrew itself as they came nigh, and left the spots where it had danced the drearier, because they had hoped to find them bright.

"Mother," said little Pearl, "the sunshine does not love you. It runs away and hides itself, because it is afraid of something on your bosom. Now see! There it is, playing, a good way off. Stand you here, and let me run and catch it. I am but a child. It will not flee from me, for I wear nothing on my bosom yet!"

"Nor ever will, my child, I hope," said Hester.

"And why not, mother?" asked Pearl, stopping short, just at the beginning of her race. "Will not it come of its own accord, when I am a woman grown?"

"Run away, child," answered her mother, "and catch the sunshine! It will soon be gone."

Pearl set forth, at a great pace, and, as Hester smiled to perceive, did actually catch the sunshine, and stood laughing in the midst of it, all brightened by its splendor, and scintillating with the vivacity excited by rapid motion. The light lingered about the lonely child, as if glad of such a playmate, until her mother had drawn almost nigh enough to step into the magic circle too.

"It will go now!" said Pearl, shaking her head.

"See!" answered Hester, smiling. "Now I can stretch out my hand, and grasp some of it."

As she attempted to do so, the sunshine vanished; or, to judge from the bright expression that was dancing on Pearl's features, her mother could have

92

fancied that the child had absorbed it into herself, and would give it forth again, with a gleam about her path, as they should plunge into some gloomier shade. There was no other attribute that so much impressed her with a sense of new and untransmitted vigor in Pearl's nature, as this never-failing vivacity of spirits; she had not the disease of sadness, which almost all children, in these latter days, inherit, with the scrofula, from the troubles of their ancestors. Perhaps this too was a disease, and but the reflex of the wild energy with which Hester had fought against her sorrows before Pearl's birth. It was certainly a doubtful charm, imparting a hard, metallic lustre to the child's character. She wanted— what some people want throughout life—a grief that should deeply touch her, and thus humanize and make her capable of sympathy. But there was time enough yet for little Pearl!

"Come, my child!" said Hester, looking about her from the spot where Pearl had stood still in the sunshine. "We will sit down a little way within the wood, and rest ourselves."

"I am not aweary, mother," replied the little girl. "But you may sit down, if you will tell me a story meanwhile."

"A story, child!" said Hester. "And about what?"

"Oh, a story about the Black Man!" answered Pearl, taking hold of her mother's gown, and looking up, half earnestly, half mischievously, into her face. "How he haunts this forest, and carries a book with him,—a big, heavy book, with iron clasps; and how this ugly Black Man offers his book and an iron pen to every body that meets him here among the trees; and they are to write their names with their own blood. And then he sets his mark on their bosoms! Didst thou ever meet the Black Man, mother?"

"And who told you this story, Pearl?" asked her mother, recognizing a common superstition of the period.

"It was the old dame in the chimney-corner, at the house where you watched last night," said the child. "But she fancied me asleep while she was talking of it. She said that a thousand and a thousand people had met him here, and had written in his book, and have his mark on them. And that ugly-tempered lady, old Mistress Hibbins, was one. And, mother, the old dame said that this scarlet letter was the Black Man's mark on thee, and that it glows like a red flame when thou meetest him at midnight, here in the dark wood. Is it true, mother? And dost thou go to meet him in the night-time?"

"Didst thou ever awake, and find thy mother gone?" asked Hester.

"Not that I remember," said the child. "If thou fearest to leave me in our cottage, thou mightest take me along with thee. I would very gladly go! But, mother, tell me now! Is there such a Black Man? And didst thou ever meet him? And is this his mark?"

"Wilt thou let me be at peace, if I once tell thee?" asked her mother.

"Yes, if thou tellest me all," answered Pearl.

"Once in my life I met the Black Man!" said her mother. "This scarlet letter is his mark!"

1. How, specifically, is the forest like the "moral wilderness" in which Hester and Dimmesdale have been wandering? What words and phrases develop this comparison?

2. What is Pearl's tone when she tells her mother that the sunshine "will not flee from me, for I wear nothing on my bosom yet"?

3. What does the sunshine symbolize in this passage? Does it symbolize more than one thing?

4. In what way might Pearl's "never-failing vivacity of spirits" be a disease? Why is her vivacity a "doubtful charm"?

5. What is Hester's tone when she tells Pearl that "once in my life I met the Black Man" and that "this scarlet letter is his mark"? How does the rest of the scene lead up to this declaration?

Passage 12

So speaking, she undid the clasp that fastened the scarlet letter, and, taking it from her bosom, threw it to a distance among the withered leaves. The mystic token alighted on the hither verge of the stream. With a hand's breadth farther flight it would have fallen into the water, and have given the little brook another woe to carry onward, besides the unintelligible tale which it still kept murmuring about. But there lay the embroidered letter, glittering like a lost jewel, which some ill-fated wanderer might pick up, and thenceforth be haunted by strange phantoms of guilt, sinkings of the heart, and unaccountable misfortune.

The stigma gone, Hester heaved a long, deep sigh, in which the burden of shame and anguish departed from her spirit. O exquisite relief! She had not known the weight, until she felt the freedom! By another impulse, she took off the formal cap that confined her hair; and down it fell upon her shoulders, dark and rich, with at once a shadow and a light in its abundance, and imparting the charm of softness to her features. There played around her mouth, and beamed out of her eyes, a radiant and tender smile, that seemed gushing from the very heart of womanhood. A crimson flush was glowing on her check, that had been long so pale. Her sex, her youth, and the whole richness of her beauty, came back from what men call the irrevocable past, and clustered themselves, with her maiden hope, and a happiness before unknown, within the magic circle of this hour. And, as if the gloom of the earth and sky had been but the effluence of these two mortal hearts, it vanished with their sorrow. All at once, as with a sudden smile of heaven, forth burst the sunshine, pouring a very flood into the obscure forest, gladdening each green leaf, transmuting the yellow fallen ones to gold, and gleaming adown the gray trunks of the solemn trees. The objects that had made a shadow hitherto, embodied the brightness now. The course of the little brook might be traced by its merry gleam afar into the wood's heart of mystery, which had become a mystery of joy.

Such was the sympathy of Nature—that wild, heathen Nature of the forest, never subjugated by human law, nor illumined by higher truth—with the bliss of these two spirits! Love, whether newly born, or aroused from a deathlike slumber, must always create a sunshine, filling the heart so full of radiance, that it overflows upon the outward world. Had the forest still kept its gloom, it would have been bright in Hester's eyes, and bright in Arthur Dimmesdale's!

1. Does the first paragraph suggest that Hester is doing right or wrong when she casts off the scarlet letter? What specific words and phrases contribute to this impression?

2. Why, after removing the scarlet letter from her bosom, does Hester let down her hair?

3. Why does Hawthorne set this climactic scene in the forest?

4. Does the narrator approve or disapprove of the "wild, heathen Nature of the forest"? What details in the passage make this evident?

5. In this passage, how does Hawthorne foreshadow the end of this period of happiness?

Passage 13

"Were it not better," said he, "that you use my poor skill to-night? Verily, dear sir, we must take pains to make you strong and vigorous for this occasion of the Election discourse. The people look for great things from you; apprehending that another year may come about, and find their pastor gone."

"Yea, to another world," replied the minister, with pious resignation. "Heaven grant it be a better one; for, in good sooth, I hardly think to tarry with my flock through the flitting seasons of another year! But, touching your medicine, kind Sir, in my present frame of body, I need it not."

"I joy to hear it," answered the physician. "It may be that my remedies, so long administered in vain, begin now to take due effect. Happy man were I, and well deserving of New England's gratitude, could I achieve this cure!"

"I thank you from my heart, most watchful friend," said the Reverend Mr. Dimmesdale, with a solemn smile. "I thank you, and can but requite your good deeds with my prayers."

"A good man's prayers are golden recompense!" rejoined old Roger Chillingworth, as he took his leave. "Yea, they are the current gold coin of the New Jerusalem, with the King's own mint-mark on them!"

1. What is the tone of this conversation between Dimmesdale and Chillingworth? What is the surface meaning? What is the underlying meaning?

2. What is Dimmesdale thinking when he speaks of "another" and "better" world? What does he want Chillingworth to understand?

3. What does Chillingworth mean when he hopes that his "remedies" will "begin now to take due effect"? What does he want Dimmesdale to understand?

4. The verb *requite* can mean either to make repayment or to avenge. Which definition is closer to Dimmesdale's intention when he says to Chillingworth, "I thank you, and can but requite your good deeds with my prayers"?

5. Why does Chillingworth end the conversation by saying that "a good man's prayers are golden recompense"? Does he want Dimmesdale to think that he considers him a good man?

Passage 14

This vocal organ was in itself a rich endowment; insomuch that a listener, comprehending nothing of the language in which the preacher spoke, might still have been swayed to and fro by the mere tone and cadence. Like all other music, it breathed passion and pathos, and emotions high or tender, in a tongue native to the human heart, wherever educated. Muffled as the sound was by its passage through the church-walls, Hester Prynne listened with such intentness, and sympathized so intimately, that the sermon had throughout a meaning for her, entirely apart from its indistinguishable words. These, perhaps, if more distinctly heard, might have been only a grosser medium, and have clogged the spiritual sense. Now she caught the low undertone, as of the wind sinking down to repose itself; then ascended with it, as it rose through progressive gradations of sweetness and power, until its volume seemed to envelop her with an atmosphere of awe and solemn grandeur. And yet, majestic as the voice sometimes became, there was for ever in it an essential character of plaintiveness. A loud or low expression of anguish,—the whisper, or the shriek, as it might be conceived, of suffering humanity, that touched a sensibility in every bosom! At times this deep strain of pathos was all that could be heard, and scarcely heard, sighing amid a desolate silence. But even when the minister's voice grew high and commanding,—when it gushed irrepressibly upward,—when it assumed its utmost breadth and power, so overfilling the church as to burst its way through the solid walls and diffuse itself in the open air,—still, if the auditor listened intently, and for the purpose, he could detect the same cry of pain. What was it? The complaint of a human heart, sorrow-laden, perchance guilty, telling its secret, whether of guilt or sorrow, to the great heart of mankind; beseeching its sympathy or forgiveness,—at every moment,—in each accent,—and never in vain! It was this profound and continual undertone that gave the clergyman his most appropriate power.

1. What does the narrator achieve by separating the meaning of Dimmesdale's words from their effect on his audience? Why does the narrator compare Dimmesdale's voice to music?

2. In this passage, what is the effect of the long sentences with many clauses?

3. Why does the narrator say that Dimmesdale's voice stirred emotion in the "human heart, wherever educated"? What is the meaning of this qualification? In what ways must the human heart be "educated"?

4. What does the narrator mean by saying "this profound and continual undertone" is what "gave the clergyman his most appropriate power"? What makes this power "appropriate," according to the narrator?

Passage 15

With a convulsive motion, he tore away the ministerial band from before his breast. It was revealed! But it were irreverent to describe that revelation. For an instant, the gaze of the horror-stricken multitude was concentrated on the ghastly miracle; while the minister stood with a flush of triumph in his face, as one who, in the crisis of acutest pain, had won a victory. Then, down he sank upon the scaffold! Hester partly raised him, and supported his head against her bosom. Old Roger Chillingworth knelt down beside him, with a blank, dull countenance, out of which the life seemed to have departed.

1. What does the word "convulsive" suggest about Dimmesdale's mental and emotional state?

2. Why does the narrator say "it were irreverent to describe that revelation"?

3. What is the effect of putting the words "ghastly miracle" together?

4. What is the effect of ending the passage with Chillingworth kneeling down beside Dimmesdale after Dimmesdale sinks down onto the scaffold? What similarities and differences between the two men are suggested in this paragraph?

5. Why does it seem as if the life departs from Chillingworth's face when Dimmesdale reveals himself?

Passage 16

After many days, when time sufficed for the people to arrange their thoughts in reference to the foregoing scene, there was more than one account of what had been witnessed on the scaffold.

Most of the spectators testified to having seen, on the breast of the unhappy minister, a SCARLET LETTER—the very semblance of that worn by Hester Prynne—imprinted in the flesh. As regarded its origin, there were various explanations, all of which must necessarily have been conjectural. Some affirmed that the Reverend Mr. Dimmesdale, on the very day when Hester Prynne first wore her ignominious badge, had begun a course of penance,—which he afterwards, in so many futile methods, followed out,—by inflicting a hideous torture on himself. Others contended that the stigma had not been produced until a long time subsequent, when old Roger Chillingworth, being a potent necromancer, had caused it to appear, through the agency of magic and poisonous drugs. Others, again,—and those best able to appreciate the minister's peculiar sensibility, and the wonderful operation of his spirit upon the body,—whispered their belief, that the awful symbol was the effect of the ever active tooth of remorse, gnawing from the inmost heart outwardly, and at last manifesting Heaven's dreadful judgment by the visible presence of the letter. The reader may choose among these theories. We have thrown all the light we could acquire upon the portent, and would gladly, now that it has done its office, erase its deep print out of our own brain, where long meditation has fixed it in very undesirable distinctness.

1. What is the effect of the narrator's telling us that there is "more than one account" of what happened on the scaffold?

2. Does the narrator appear to endorse any of the interpretations offered? What words or phrases support a particular interpretation?

3. What is the narrator's tone when he says that "the reader may choose among these theories"?

4. Why does the narrator shift to the first person at the end of this passage?

5. Why does the narrator want to erase the memory of the scarlet letter?

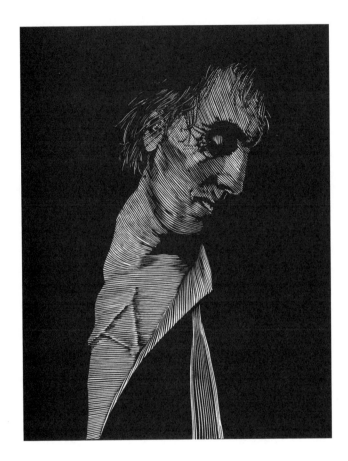

The Scarlet Letter

Suggestions for Writing

✦

Writing about literature is best thought of as an extension of reading
and discussion, as readers return to unresolved questions or investigate unexplored
avenues of inquiry. Readers may also learn and retain more by articulating
their ideas carefully and thoroughly in written form.

Analytical Writing

1. "The Minister's Black Veil" was published in 1836, fourteen years before *The Scarlet Letter*. In what ways are Hooper and Dimmesdale similar? In what ways are they different? What do the endings of the two stories reveal about each man's character?

2. Both Arthur Dimmesdale from *The Scarlet Letter* and the Reverend Mr. Hooper from "The Minister's Black Veil" exert enormous influence over their congregations. Write an essay analyzing the power of the preacher in Puritan times. Consider the techniques of persuasion used by Jonathan Edwards in "Sinners in the Hands of an Angry God."

3. Hawthorne uses symbols throughout *The Scarlet Letter* to represent a variety of themes and ideas. Write an essay analyzing two or three important symbols (e.g., the letter, the scaffold, the brook) and explore how they contribute to the meaning of the novel.

4. Write an essay analyzing the theme of sin and atonement in *The Scarlet Letter*. Focusing on at least two of the novel's main characters, compare and contrast their sins and their methods of atonement.

5. Write a character analysis of Roger Chillingworth/Prynne. How responsible is he for his actions? Are there any mitigating circumstances? Does Hawthorne want us to feel any sympathy for him?

6. Consider the parallels between Roger Chillingworth and Ethan Brand. In what ways are their quests similar? Does Hawthorne want us to sympathize with either one of them?

7. Analyze the opposition that Hawthorne creates between the town and the forest. Why do several of the novel's important scenes take place in the forest? What roles do nature and wilderness play in the novel? What is Hawthorne's view of the forest as opposed to the town?

8. Write an essay analyzing how Hawthorne portrays women and their place in society in *The Scarlet Letter*, paying close attention to the narrator's comments about Hester's ideas and actions.

9. Analyze the conflict that Hawthorne creates between the rights of an individual and the individual's responsibility to the community. Is Hester, as the heroine of the novel, a nonconformist or conformist? Do Hester's ideas and actions suggest that the individual is more important than the community or that the community is more important than the individual?

10. Write an essay that analyzes the novel's depiction of Puritan society. What elements of this society are portrayed favorably? What elements are portrayed unfavorably? On the whole, does the narrator suggest that it is superior or inferior to the society of his own time?

Creative/Personal Writing

1. Create a list of "Unpardonable Sins" for today's world. Write a story in which the main character has an understandable reason for committing one of these sins. Explain how other characters in your story respond to the main character.

2. Imagine that during his search for the "Unpardonable Sin," Ethan Brand came upon Hester Prynne, Roger Chillingworth, or Arthur Dimmesdale. Write the dialogue that might occur between the two characters. On which points would they agree and disagree? Try to imitate the speech patterns that Hawthorne uses.

3. Go to a yard sale or a secondhand shop and buy an item that catches your attention (or find an interesting object at home that you have never noticed before). Write a story in which the object you found is a central symbol, modeling your tale on the Custom House chapter from *The Scarlet Letter.*

4. Imagine that Hester keeps a diary and that she has just returned from her meeting with Dimmesdale in the forest. In Hester's voice, write the entry that describes her thoughts and feelings about the encounter.

5. As Roger Chillingworth, write a letter to Pearl explaining why you were so relentless in your pursuit of Dimmesdale and why you left your money to her.

6. Imagine Pearl returning to Massachusetts on the occasion of Hester's death. Write the eulogy she might deliver at Hester's funeral.

7. In *The Scarlet Letter,* Hawthorne is writing about a time over 100 years before his own. Write a brief story set 100 years ago, and use your narrator to suggest your attitude toward that time.

8. Are people ever justified in breaking vows, as Hester and Dimmesdale do? Write a personal essay arguing under what conditions (if any) one might be justified in breaking a promise to another person.

Background and Context

These selections, including sermons from the Puritan preachers
of colonial America, historical accounts of the Salem
witchcraft trials, and early reviews of the novel, offer insights into
the seventeenth-century setting of The Scarlet Letter
and the nineteenth-century era of its author.

The Puritans

PAGE 112: Portrait (circa 1674) of Elizabeth and Mary Freake, wife and daughter of John Freake, a wealthy Boston merchant and attorney. This is one of the few portraits that survive from late-seventeenth-century New England.

LEFT: John Winthrop (1588–1649) served as governor of the Massachusetts Bay Colony for fifteen of the colony's first twenty years.

BELOW: This 1677 map of New England, called "The White Hills Map," was the first map to be engraved and printed in America. (Map is oriented with north to the right.)

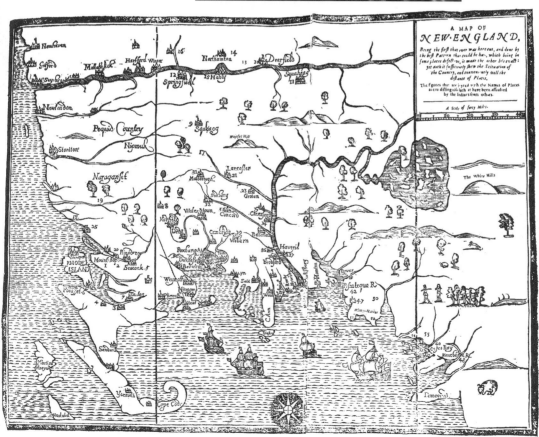

ABOVE: This reconstruction of
Plymouth shows how the first
New England settlement would
have appeared circa 1627.

LEFT: Old Trinity Church (circa
1675) near Cambridge, Maryland,
was restored in 1960 with typical
seventeenth-century-style box
pews and high north pulpit.

These embroidered gloves (circa 1650), belonging to Governor
John Leverett (1616–1679) of the Massachusetts Bay Company,
show the style of intricate embroidery Hawthorne refers to in his
description of the scarlet A. Sumptuary laws in seventeenth-
century Massachusetts dictated that clothing must be "suitable
to the estate or quality of each person."

THE DIARY OF MICHAEL WIGGLESWORTH

Michael Wigglesworth

February 1653

Remembered today primarily as the author of *The Day of Doom* (1662), a lengthy poem about the Last Judgment, Michael Wigglesworth (1631–1705) was part of the group of devout Pilgrims who first settled in New England. He became a minister after attending Harvard College (founded as a Puritan seminary) and teaching there for several years. He wrote most of the existing diary, which covers the years 1653–1657, while teaching at Harvard.

If the unloving carriages of my pupils can goe so to my heart as they doe; how then doe my vain thoughts, my detestable pride, my unnatural filthy lust that are so oft and even this day in some measure stirring in me how do these griev my lord Jesus that loves me infinitely more then I do them? Do I take it heavily that my love is so lightly made of? ah! lord Jesus how fearful is my despizing of thy dying love, of thy love in giving me thy self after thou seemedst to haue cast me of for ever? ah! I cannot love thee, not fear to sin against thee, although thou exercise me with such crosses, as again this day, wherein I may read my owne ill carriages toward thee. And dost thou yet make any beam of thy love break out toward me, after any fears? Nay have so oft and so long comforted my self with thy love amidst my daily sins. The enmity and contrariety of my heart to seeking thee in earnest, with my want of dear affection to thee, these make me affraid. but thou did giue me thy self in the Lords supper, thou dist giue me a heart (though vile) to lay hold of the desiring all from thee. and this giues me hope. blessed be thy name.

Pride and vain thoughts again prevail over me to the grief of my god. clense me, o lord, when shall it once be? I had opportunity (purposely takeing of it) to discourse with one of my pupils much of the things of god; as also with another out of the colledge whom I went to visit, who spake something to me about his spiritual condition, the lord helping me to speak much to him again with some affection: the Lord bless it to them both. My pupil was John Haines. I spoke to them both what a blessed thing it was to serve and seek the Lord.

February 7, 1653

peevishness vain thoughts and especially pride still prevails in me. I cannot think one good thought, I cannot do any thing for god but presently pride gets hould of me. but I feel a need of christ's blood to wash me from the sins of my best dutys and from all that deadness of heart, and want of spirit for god this day. I find my heart prone to take secret pleasure in thinking how much I do for others' good: but Lord how little of it is done for the. I fear there is much sensuality and doting upon the creature in my pursuit of the good of others; I cannot seek gods glory therein but am carry'd most with pitty to man. else the Lord would hardly cross me in my endeavours and hopes: were it not to shew me, that both my labours and those persons whom I haue greatest hopes of are also vanity. Lord why is my soul glutted so with my owne projects that I oft times feel little need of thy self   Small cause then to be proud of the love I bear to these which thou hast given me when by love to them I cease loving of thee. Lord heal this wound this day.

February 15, 1653

Pride I feel still again and again abounding, self-admiration, though destroying my self daly.   god gracious and bountifull in bestowing in directing me and mine, but I unthankfully wickedly making gods gifts subservient to my vain glory.   ah Lord I am vile, I desire to abhor my self (o that I could!) before the for these things.

April 3–4, 1653

Vain thoughts break in upon me. My soul cant get over a disconsolate troubled devoted frame in reference to my pupils and other troubles concerning   Ah Lord let me see thy face that will fill up all my emptiness and the dissatisfaction I find in the creature. I wait and oh that I could long for thy salvation O where are thy tender compassions and bowel mercies which I have been comforted with when low O hide not thy face from me O thou that hath delivered my feet out of the miry clay O thou that hath brought me out of the iron furnace to whom I have sung songs of praise.

O wretch that I am my iniquity like clay and fetters holds me down that the good I would do I cant the evil I would not do that do I. Nay I feel my heart apt secretly to give way to my vain thoughts in holy duties and glued as it were to my sensuality or love to the creature full of hope since and cant get over sinking and disquietments of spirit (because things go not well with my pupils) and as for pride why it overcomes me in holiest duties where there should be most abasement   The Lord has given me several opportunities of grace more than ordinary this week as one lecture and two private meetings but my heart at both was so vile that I may even be a burden to my self.

April 5, 1653

Very much pride yet prevailes, and hypocrisy: my bodily strength ffails me so that I can scarce do any thing, but in assaying am a weariness to my self. my sins are too hard for me: my desires in reference to my journey are crost: expectations fail all is vanity. why Lord withold not now thy grace and good spirit, giving patience under thy hand, that I may be willing to miss this opportunity and still to bear my infirmitys, till thy time come when thou wilt commaund health. o assure me of thy love, and then I know all shall work for my good.

August 5, 1653

But ah how apt am I to kick with the heel Jesurun like and lightly to esteem the rock of my salvation? how soon haue I forgotten his wonderful works? A mind distracted with a thousand vanitys sabbath dayes and week days when I should be musing off the things of god But where is my sorrow and bitter mourning for these prophanations of gods ordinances? a thing so grievous to my God. It hath bin some grief to me that I am so unprofitable a servant, that I cannot serv god in my calling aiming at his glory, and doing it as his work. I haue begged this mercy but alas! I cannot attain it, but I lose myself and my love to god amidst my multitude of occasions. My heart is hurried now this way, now that way by divers lusts; one while anxiously sollicitous, another while pleasing myself with this or that creature, this or that project, but ah! where is my walking with god, and rejoycing in the light of his countenance? And now good Lord haue mercy on me! how unfit am I to sanctify a sabbath, with such a carnal heart, such dead and dul affections, such distracting thoughts as posses and fill my mind, such a faint and feeble body? And how much more unfit to partake of a sacrament? I am affraid I shall abuse it: at least get no good by it, But the same carnal, secure, vain sensual, slouthful, proud, unbeleiving, unthankful, unfruitfull frame remain in me still. He also (even the sonns of God) is flesh; this is that which grieveth the Lord at the heart. such an one am I: oh! that I could relent and repent with hearty sorrow. And when shall it be otherwise good Lord!

when shall it once be? Thy ordinances are of thyne own appointing and in them thou wilt be sought; and wilt thou not be found? Is it invain to come to sacraments and beleiv on, and feed upon christ as given by thy self? I know it is not invain: though my sins be not yet subdued, though my wounds are yet unhealed. faithful is he who hath promised and will perform it, though I be vile. I feel dayly a spirit of whoardom in the midst of me, a heart revolting from god to the other things. But yet verily Living and dying thou art my hope, o do not fail me utterly; forsake me not o my God; but uphold me by thy right hand in following hard after thee; and let me find that it is not in vain to wait upon thee in ways of thy own appointment.

September 26, 1653

upon examination before the Lord supper I find

1. A loose and common heart that loveth vanity and frothyness.

2. A prophane heart appearing in $\left\{\begin{array}{l}\text{Distracting thoughts in holy dutys}\\\text{wearines of them through}\\\text{slouth and carnality}\end{array}\right.$

3. A proud heart.

4. An unbelieving heart. which questeons Gods love, which cannot wait his time which cannot trust his providence without distracting cares and overwhelming disquietments.

5. An hard heart that cannot be so deeply affected with my sins and spiritual wants, as with my outward troubles this maketh me affraid.

6. A sensual. heart that sometimes can se no glory in heavenly things, no nor in heaven it self.

7. An unthankful heart

8. A heart full of spiritual whoardoms revolting from the Lord to some vanity [or] other every day

At the Lords supper god helpt me to desire, and close with whole christ as prophet priest and King. And though sathan cast objection into my mind because I was no member of this particular church, nor yet recommended hither by Cambridge church; yet I strive against them and said Lord I do beleiv help my unbeleif; and o that I might go away and sin no more against so gracious a god so sweet a saviour

September 29, 1653

I stil find a spirit of pride, and a spirit of whoardom which is restless in roaving after something in the creature; sometimes after this or that study, but I cannot so earnestly desire after prayer, meditation, reading the word   this is a body of death and a sorrowful burden to me Lord thou knowest.

February 12–13, 1654

I find pride, and sensual outgoing of heart one while, and discouragement another while apt to prevail over me.   and fleshly lusts too are sometimes too strong for me. O wretched man that I am! which way so ever I turn me.   unfit to live becaus sinful at present and overborn, overpowered by corruptions so many.   unfit to dy because sensual and not savouring the things of another world: because myne iniquitys separate between me and my god and hide his face from me.   sorrows I meet with and temptations, and more I deserve than I feel, and therefore wel may I fear more.   oh I haue a carnal secure, proud, prophane, unbeleiving heart! that I wil complain off heavenly father, and not off thee. Thou art good, I am evil, thou art faithful I am unfaithful in the covenant.   oh I am ashamed that I dishonour my fathers hous so by feeding upon husks.   that I wrong and griev my head and husband so by not loving and delighting in his presence; by my liking other loves more than him ah Lord! I pul down evils upon others as wel as my self. Sicknesses, death of godly ones, wants, divisions have not my sins a hand in these miserys?   oh Lord I am affraid of thy judgements upon my self and others. But spare thy people. I do beseech thee whatever become of me.

CHRIST'S FIDELITY

Deodat Lawson

To our honored magistrates, here present this day, to inquire into these things, give me leave, much honored, to offer one word to your consideration. Do all that in you lies to check and rebuke Satan; endeavoring, by all ways and means that are according to the rule of God, to discover his instruments in these horrid operations. You are concerned in the civil government of this people, being invested with power by their Sacred Majesties, under this glorious Jesus (the King and Governor of his church), for the supporting of Christ's kingdom against all oppositions of Satan's kingdom and his instruments. Being ordained of God to such a station (Rom. 13:1), we entreat you, bear not the sword in vain, as verse 4; but approve yourselves a terror of and punishment to evildoers, and a praise to them that do well (1 Pet. 2:14); ever remembering that ye judge not for men, but for the Lord (2 Chron. 19:6); and, as his promise is, so our prayer shall be for you, without ceasing, that he would be with you in the judgment, as he that can and will direct, assist, and reward you. Follow the example of the upright Job (Job 29:16): Be a father to the poor; to these poor afflicted persons, in pitiful and painful endeavors to help them; and the cause that seems to be so dark, as you know not how to determine it, do your utmost, in the use of all regular means, to search it out.

Deodat Lawson (fl. 1680–1698) was the minister of Salem Village immediately before the witchcraft accusations. This selection is taken from the sermon addressing the role of the magistrates as enforcers of civil and divine law that Lawson published in 1693. He preached the original version in Salem on March 24, 1692.

⚬⚬⚬

Matthew Hopkins of Essex, England, the son of a Puritan minister and a self-proclaimed witch finder, was responsible for the deaths of more than 200 people. This illustration is the frontispiece from John Geule's *Select Cases of Conscience Touching Witches and Witchcraft* (1646), a small volume that exposed Hopkins's methods as false. According to some accounts, Hopkins was put to one of his own tests for witchcraft: upon being cast into a river, he floated and was therefore declared to be a wizard and put to death.

THE WONDERS OF THE INVISIBLE WORLD

Cotton Mather

A People of God in the Devil's Territories

A skillful preacher and eminent theologian, Cotton Mather (1663–1728) wrote and published more than 400 works. Mather's most significant work was a history of the New England churches, *Magnalia Christi Americana* (1702). In May 1692, as the Salem witchcraft trials began, Mather was asked by the judges to write a formal summary of the proceedings. In this selection, Mather describes the case against the accused.

The New Englanders are a people of God settled in those, which were once the Devil's territories; and it may easily be supposed that the Devil was exceedingly disturbed, when he perceived such a people here accomplishing the promise of old made unto our blessed Jesus, that He should have the utmost parts of the earth for His possession. There was not a greater uproar among the Ephesians, when the Gospel was first brought among them, than there was among the powers of the air (after whom those Ephesians walked) when first the silver trumpets of the Gospel here made the joyful sound. The Devil thus irritated, immediately tried all sorts of methods to overturn this poor plantation: and so much of the church, as was fled into this wilderness, immediately found the serpent cast out of his mouth a flood for the carrying of it away. I believe that never were more satanical devices used for the unsettling of any people under the sun, than what have been employed for the extirpation of the vine, which God has here planted, casting out the heathen, and preparing a room before it, and causing it to take deep root, and fill the land, so that it sent its boughs unto the Atlantic Sea eastward, and its branches unto the Connecticut River westward, and the hills were covered with the shadow thereof. But all those attempts of hell have hitherto been abortive; many an Ebenezer has been erected unto the praise of God by his poor people here, and having obtained help from God, we continue to this day. Wherefore the Devil is now making one attempt more upon us; an attempt more difficult, more surprising, more snarled with unintelligible circumstances than any that we have hitherto encountered; an attempt so critical, that if we get well through, we shall soon enjoy halcyon days with all the vultures of hell trodden under our feet. He has wanted his incarnate legions to persecute us, as the people of God have in the other hemisphere been persecuted; he has therefore drawn forth his more spiritual ones to make an attack upon us. We have been advised by some credible Christians yet alive that a malefactor, accused of witchcraft as well as murder, and executed in this place more than forty years ago, did then give notice of a horrible plot against the country by witchcraft, and a foundation of witchcraft then laid, which, if it were not seasonably discovered, would probably blow up and pull down all the churches in the country. And we have now with horror seen the discovery of such a witchcraft! An army of devils is horribly broke in upon the place which is the center and after a sort, the first born of our English settlements, and the houses of the good people there are filled with the doleful shrieks of their children and servants, tormented by invisible hands, with tortures altogether preternatural. After the mischiefs there endeavored and since in part conquered, the terrible plague of evil angels hath made its progress into some other places, where other persons have been in like manner diabolically handled. These our poor afflicted neighbors, quickly after they become infected and infested with these demons, arrive to a capacity of discerning those which they conceive the shapes of their troublers; and notwithstanding the great and just suspicion that the demons might impose the shapes of innocent persons in their spectral exhibitions upon the sufferers (which may perhaps prove no small part of the witch

plot in the issue), yet many of the persons thus represented, being examined, several of them have been convicted of a very damnable witchcraft: yea, more than one twenty have confessed that they have signed unto a book, which the Devil showed them, and engaged in his hellish design of bewitching and ruining our land. We know not, at least I know not, how far the delusions of Satan may be interwoven into some circumstances of the confessions; but one would think all the rules of understanding human affairs are at an end, if after so many most voluntary harmonious confessions, made by intelligent persons of all ages in sundry towns at several times, we must not believe the main strokes wherein those confessions all agree: especially when we have a thousand preternatural things every day before our eyes, wherein the confessors do acknowledge their concernment and give demonstration of their being so concerned. If the devils

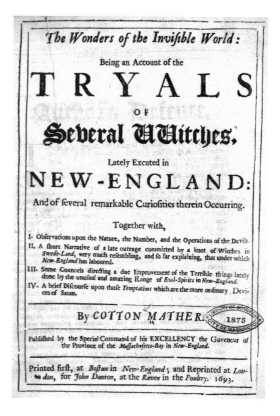

The Wonders of the Invisible World:

Being an Account of the

TRYALS

OF

Several Witches,

Lately Excuted in

NEW-ENGLAND:

And of several remarkable Curiosities therein Occurring.

Together with,

I. Observations upon the Nature, the Number, and the Operations of the Devils.

II. A short Narrative of a late outrage committed by a knot of Witches in Swede-Land, very much resembling, and so far explaining, that under which New-England has laboured.

III. Some Councels directing a due Improvement of the Terrible things lately done by the unusual and amazing Range of Evil-Spirits in New-England.

IV. A brief Discourse upon those Temptations which are the more ordinary Devices of Satan.

By COTTON MATHER.

Published by the Special Command of his EXCELLENCY the Govenour of the Province of the Massachusetts-Bay in New-England.

Printed first, at Boston in New-England ; and Reprinted at London, for John Dunton, at the Raven in the Poultry. 1693.

now can strike the minds of men with any poisons of so fine a composition and operation that scores of innocent people shall unite in confessions of a crime, which we see actually committed, it is a thing prodigious beyond the wonders of the former ages, and it threatens no less than a sort of a dissolution upon the world. Now, by these confessions 'tis agreed that the Devil has made a dreadful knot of witches in the country, and by the help of witches has dreadfully increased that knot; that these witches have driven a trade of commissioning their confederate spirits to do all sorts of mischiefs to the neighbors, whereupon there have ensued such mischievous consequences upon the bodies and estates of the neighborhood, as could not otherwise be accounted for: yea, that at prodigious witch meetings, the wretches have proceeded so far as to concert and consult the methods of rooting out the Christian religion from this country, and setting up instead of it perhaps a more gross diabolism than ever the world saw before. And yet it will be a thing little short of miracle, if in so spread a business as this, the Devil should not get in some of his juggles to confound the discovery of all the rest.

ANNALS OF SALEM: LAWS GOVERNING ADULTERY

Joseph B. Felt

May 5th, 1694

The Reverend Joseph B. Felt (1789–1869) first published his two-volume history *The Annals of Salem* in 1827 and 1828.

A memorial was received, signed by many clergymen, desiring the Legislature to enact laws against prevailing iniquities. Among such laws, passed this session, were two against Adultery and Polygamy. Those guilty of the first crime were to sit an hour on the gallows with ropes about their necks, be severely whipped not above forty stripes, and forever after wear a capital A, two inches long, cut out of cloth colored differently from their clothes, and sewed on the arms, or back parts of their garments so as always to be seen when they were about. The other crime, stated with suitable exceptions, was punishable with death.

SINNERS IN THE HANDS OF AN ANGRY GOD

Their foot shall slide in due time. (Deut. 32:35)

Jonathan Edwards

Application

The use of this awful subject may be for awakening unconverted persons in this congregation. This that you have heard is the case of every one of you that are out of Christ. That world of misery, that lake of burning brimstone is extended abroad under you. There is the dreadful pit of the glowing flames of the wrath of God; there is hell's wide gaping mouth open; and you have nothing to stand upon, nor any thing to take hold of; there is nothing between you and hell but the air; it is only the power and mere pleasure of God that holds you up.

You probably are not sensible of this; you find you are kept out of hell, but do not see the hand of God in it; but look at other things, as the good state of your bodily constitution, your care of your own life, and the means you use for your own preservation. But indeed these things are nothing; if God should withdraw His hand, they would avail no more to keep you from falling, than the thin air to hold up a person that is suspended in it.

Your wickedness makes you as it were heavy as lead, and to tend downwards with great weight and pressure toward hell; and if God should let you go, you would immediately sink and swiftly descend and plunge into the bottomless gulf, and your healthy constitution, and your own care and prudence, and best contrivance, and all your righteousness, would have no more influence to uphold you and keep you out of hell, than a spider's web would have to stop a fallen rock. Were it not for the sovereign pleasure of God, the earth would not bear you one moment; for you are a burden to it; the creation groans with you; the creature is made subject to the bondage of your corruption, not willingly; the sun does not willingly shine upon you to give you light to serve sin and Satan; the earth does not willingly yield her increase to satisfy your lusts; nor is it willingly a stage for your wickedness to be acted upon; the air does not willingly serve you for breath to maintain the flame of life in your vitals, while you spend your life in the service of God's enemies. God's creatures are good, and were made for men to serve God with, and do not willingly subserve to any other purpose, and groan when they are abused to purposes so directly contrary to their nature and end. And the world would spew you out, were it not for the sovereign hand of Him who hath subjected it in hope. There are black clouds of

From the 1720s to the 1740s, the American colonies experienced the Great Awakening, a time of religious revival marked by mass conversions to Christianity. Jonathan Edwards (1703–1758), the Yale-educated pastor of Northampton, Massachusetts (which had the largest church outside of Boston), was perhaps the most famous preacher of the time and was responsible for the conversion of thousands of New Englanders. This selection from "Sinners in the Hands of an Angry God," the most famous sermon in American history, demonstrates the fervor of the era and the power wielded by Puritan preachers.

God's wrath now hanging directly over your heads, full of the dreadful storm, and big with thunder; and were it not for the restraining hand of God, it would immediately burst forth upon you. The sovereign pleasure of God, for the present, stays His rough wind; otherwise it would come with fury, and your destruction would come like a whirlwind, and you would be like the chaff of the summer threshing floor.

The wrath of God is like great waters that are dammed for the present; they increase more and more, and rise higher and higher, till an outlet is given; and the longer the stream is stopped, the more rapid and mighty is its course when once it is let loose. It is true that judgment against your evil works has not been

This illustration by W. L. Sheppard, originally captioned "Whipping Quakers Through the Streets of Boston," depicts the zealous Puritans' intolerance for Quaker beliefs.

executed hitherto; the floods of God's vengeance have been withheld; but your guilt in the meantime is constantly increasing, and you are every day treasuring up more wrath; the waters are constantly rising, and waxing more and more mighty; and there is nothing but the mere pleasure of God that holds the waters back, that are unwilling to be stopped, and press hard to go forward. If God should only withdraw His hand from the floodgate, it would immediately fly open, and the fiery floods of the fierceness and wrath of God, would rush forth with inconceivable fury, and would come upon you with omnipotent power; and if your strength were ten thousand times greater than it is, yea, ten thousand times greater than the strength of the stoutest, sturdiest devil in hell, it would be nothing to withstand or endure it.

The bow of God's wrath is bent, and the arrow made ready on the string, and justice bends the arrow at your heart, and strains the bow, and it is nothing but the mere pleasure of God, and that of an angry God, without any promise or obligation at all, that keeps the arrow one moment from being made drunk with your blood. Thus all you that never passed under a great change of heart, by the mighty power of the Spirit of God upon your souls, all you that were never born again, and made new creatures, and raised from being dead in sin, to a state of new, and before altogether unexperienced light and life, are in the hands of an angry God. However you may have reformed your life in many things, and may have had religious affections, and may keep up a form of religion in your families and closets, and in the house of God, it is nothing but His mere pleasure that keeps you from being this moment swallowed up in everlasting destruction. However unconvinced you may now be of the truth of what you hear, by and by you will be fully convinced of it. Those that are gone from being in the like circumstances with you see that it was so with them; for destruction came suddenly upon most of them; when they expected nothing of it and while they were saying, peace and safety: now they see that those things on which they depended for peace and safety, were nothing but thin air and empty shadows.

The God that holds you over the pit of hell, much as one holds a spider or some loathsome insect over the fire, abhors you, and is dreadfully provoked: His wrath toward you burns like fire; He looks upon you as worthy of nothing else but to be cast into the fire; He is of purer eyes than to bear to have you in His sight; you are ten thousand times more abominable in His eyes than the most hateful venomous serpent is in ours. You have offended Him infinitely more than ever a stubborn rebel did his prince; and yet it is nothing but His hand that holds you from falling into the fire every moment. It is to be ascribed to nothing else, that you did not go to hell the last night; that you was suffered to awake again in this world, after you closed your eyes to sleep. And there is no other reason to be given, why you have not dropped into hell since you arose in the morning, but that God's hand has held you up. There is no other reason to be given why you have not gone to hell, since you have sat here in the house of God, provoking His pure eyes by your sinful wicked manner of attending His solemn worship. Yea, there is nothing else that is to be given as a reason why you do not this very moment drop down into hell.

O sinner! Consider the fearful danger you are in: it is a great furnace of wrath, a wide and bottomless pit, full of the fire of wrath, that you are held over in the hand of that God, whose wrath is provoked and incensed as much against you, as against many of the damned in hell. You hang by a slender thread, with the flames of divine wrath flashing about it, and ready every moment to singe it, and burn it asunder; and you have no interest in any Mediator, and nothing to lay hold of to save yourself, nothing to keep off the flames of wrath, nothing of your own, nothing that you ever have done, nothing that you can do, to induce God to spare you one moment.

✐✐

Nathaniel Hawthorne's
Notebooks

THE AMERICAN NOTEBOOKS

1840–1841

To symbolize moral or spiritual disease by disease of the body; thus, when a person committed any sin, it might cause a sore to appear on the body; this to be wrought out.

1842–1843

Pearl—the English of Margaret—a pretty name for girl in a story.

A man seeks for something excellent, and seeks it in the wrong way, and in a wrong spirit, and finds something horrible—as for instance, he seeks for treasure, and finds a dead body—for the gold that somebody has hidden, and brings to light his accumulated sins.

During his lifetime, Hawthorne kept journals and notebooks where he jotted down ideas for themes, characters, and stories. The short selections that follow, taken from *The American Notebooks*, offer a glimpse of Hawthorne's early ideas for *The Scarlet Letter*. The selections from *The English Notebooks* describe the state of Hawthorne's life after the success of *The Scarlet Letter* and his last meeting with Herman Melville.

Etching of the Old Manse, by Ross Turner, from the 1882 Riverside edition of Hawthorne's *Mosses from an Old Manse*. Hawthorne and Sophia lived in the house for three years after their marriage in 1842.

The Magic Play of Sunshine, for a child's story—the sunshine circling round through a prisoner's cell, from his high and narrow window. He keeps his soul alive and cheerful by means of it, it typifying cheerfulness; and when he is released, he takes up the ray of sunshine and carries it away with him; and it enables him to discover treasures all over the world, in places where nobody else would think of looking for any.

1844–1846

The search of an investigator for the Unpardonable Sin—he at last finds it in his own heart and practice.

The trees reflected in the river—they are unconscious of a spiritual world so near them. So are we.

The Unpardonable Sin might consist in a want of love and reverence for the Human Soul; in consequence of which the investigator pried into its dark depths, not with a hope or purpose of making it better, but from a philosophical curiosity—content that it should be wicked in whatever kind or degree, and only desiring to study it out. Would not this, in other words, be the separation of the intellect from the heart?

THE ENGLISH NOTEBOOKS

A Singular Dream

December 28th [1854]—I think I have been happier, this Christmas, than ever before—by our own fireside, and with my wife and children about me. More content to enjoy what I had; less anxious for anything beyond it, in this life. My early life was perhaps a good preparation for the declining half of life, it having been such a blank that any possible thereafter would compare favorably with it. For a long, long while, I have occasionally been visited with a singular dream; and I have an impression that I have dreamed it even since I have been in England. It is that I am still at college—or, sometimes, even at school—and there is a sense that I have been there unconscionably long, and have quite

Undated illustration of Hawthorne reading to his wife and children

failed to make such progress in life as my contemporaries have; and I seem to meet some of them with a feeling of shame and depression that broods over me, when I think of it, even at this moment. This dream, recurring all through these twenty or thirty years, must be one of the effects of that heavy seclusion in which I shut myself up, for twelve years, after leaving college, when everybody moved onward and left me behind. How strange that it should come now, when I may call myself famous, and prosperous!—when I am happy, too!—still that same dream of life hopelessly a failure!

Herman Melville

November 20th [1856]—A week ago last Monday, Herman Melville came to see me at the Consulate, looking much as he used to do (a little paler, and perhaps a little sadder), in a rough outside coat, and with his characteristic gravity and reserve of manner. He had crossed from New York to Glasgow in a screw steamer, about a fortnight before, and had since been seeing Edinburgh and other interesting places. I felt rather awkward at first, because this is the first time I have met him since my ineffectual attempt to get him a consular appointment from General Pierce. However, I failed only from real lack of power to serve him, so there was no reason to be ashamed, and we soon found ourselves on pretty much our former terms of sociability and confidence. Melville has not been well, of late; he has been affected with neuralgic complaints in his head and limbs, and no doubt has suffered from too constant literary occupation, pursued without much success, latterly; and his writings, for a long while past, have indicated a morbid state of mind. So he left his place at Pittsfield, and has established his wife and family, I believe, with his father-in-law in Boston, and is thus far on his way to Constantinople. I do not wonder that he found it necessary to take an airing through the world, after so many years of toilsome pen labor and domestic life, following upon so wild and adventurous a youth as his was. I invited him to come and stay with us at Southport, as long as he might remain in this vicinity; and accordingly, he did come, the next day, taking with him, by way of baggage, the least little bit of a bundle, which, he told me, contained a nightshirt and a toothbrush. He is a person of very gentlemanly instincts in every respect, save that he is a little heterodox in the matter of clean linen.

He stayed with us from Tuesday till Thursday; and, on the intervening day, we took a pretty long walk together, and sat down in a hollow among the sand hills (sheltering ourselves from the high, cool wind) and smoked a cigar. Melville, as he always does, began to reason of Providence and futurity, and of everything that lies beyond human ken, and informed me that he had "pretty much made up his mind to be annihilated"; but still he does not seem to rest in that anticipation; and, I think, will never rest until be gets hold of a definite belief. It is strange how he persists—and has persisted ever since I knew him, and probably long before—in wandering to and fro over these deserts, as dismal and monotonous as the sand hills amid which we were sitting. He can neither believe, nor be comfortable in his unbelief; and he is too honest and courageous not to try to do one or the other. If he were a religious man, he would be one of the most truly religious and reverential; he has a very high and noble nature, and better worth immortality than most of us.

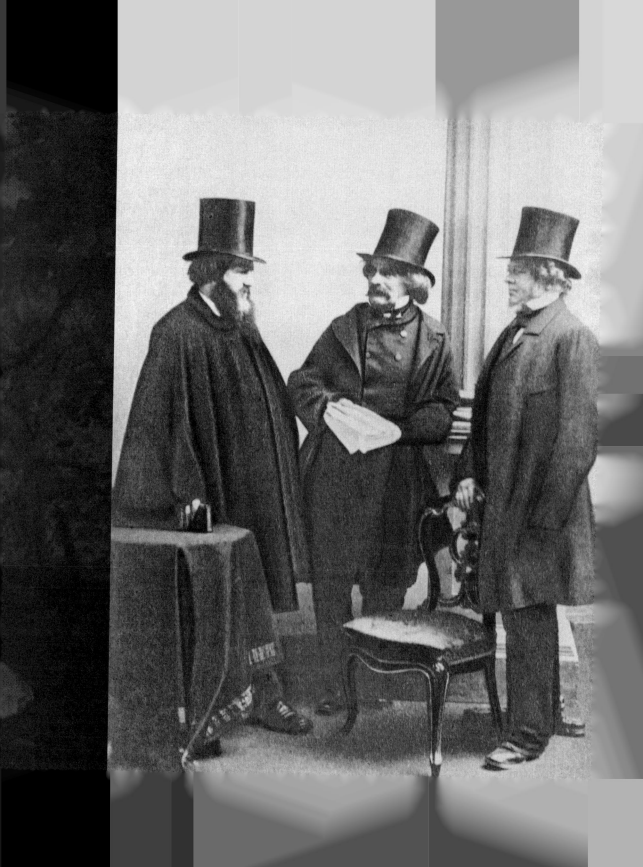

Reviews and Reactions

PAGE 134: Photograph of Hawthorne (center) with his publishers, John Fields and William Ticknor, circa 1861. Ticknor and Fields's Boston-based firm published the works of many famous American writers of the day, including Henry Wadsworth Longfellow and Robert Lowell.

LEFT: An early illustration of Hester Prynne, circa 1855

BELOW, LEFT: Lillian Gish as Hester Prynne in the 1926 silent film version of *The Scarlet Letter*, directed by Victor Sjöström

BELOW, RIGHT: "Hester Prynne," by Sigismond de Ivanowski, an early-twentieth-century illustrator

THE MADMAN'S EYES HID THE WORLD'S
MOST FIENDISH TORTURES!

A SPECTACLE OF HUMAN PASSION
AS TIMELESS AS SIN ITSELF!

ADULTERESS —
MORALITY MEANT NOTHING TO HER!
What Was The BIZARRE CURSE Of
"The Scarlet Letter"?

THE SCARLET LETTER

SPECTACULAR SCREEN VERSION OF
NATHANIEL HAWTHORNE'S
GREATEST NOVEL!

Directed by ROBERT G. VIGNOLA
Recorded by RCA SOUND SYSTEM
With a Tremendous Cast

A
SIGNATURE
FILMS
PRESENTATION

LEFT: Publicity poster for the 1965 film version of *The Scarlet Letter*, directed by Robert G. Vignola

BELOW, LEFT: Demi Moore as Hester Prynne in the 1995 film version of *The Scarlet Letter*, directed by Roland Joffe

BELOW, RIGHT: Charlayne Woodard as Hester, La Negrita, in a 1999 production of *In the Blood*, playwright Suzan-Lori Parks's modern retelling of *The Scarlet Letter*. In Parks's play, Hester is a black, homeless, single mother of five who faces racial, economic, and sexual discrimination as she tries to provide for her children.

MORBID HEARTS

Edwin Percy Whipple

This review appeared in *Graham's Magazine* 36 in May 1850.

With regard to *The Scarlet Letter,* the readers of Hawthorne might have expected an exquisitely written story, expansive in sentiment, and suggestive in characterization, but they will hardly be prepared for a novel of so much tragic interest and tragic power, so deep in thought and so condensed in style, as is here presented to them. It evinces equal genius in the region of great passions and elusive emotions, and bears on every page the evidence of a mind thoroughly alive, watching patiently the movements of morbid hearts when stirred by strange experiences, and piercing, by its imaginative power, directly through all the externals to the core of things. The fault of the book, if fault it have, is the almost morbid intensity with which the characters are realized, and the consequent lack of sufficient geniality in the delineation. A portion of the pain of the author's own heart is communicated to the reader, and although there is great pleasure received while reading the volume, the general impression left by it is not satisfying to the artistic sense. Beauty bends to power throughout the work, and therefore the power displayed is not always beautiful. There is a strange fascination to a man of contemplative genius in the psychological details of a strange crime like that which forms the plot of *The Scarlet Letter,* and he is therefore apt to become like Hawthorne, too painfully anatomical in his exhibition of them.

If there be, however, a comparative lack of relief to the painful emotions which the novel excites, owing to the intensity with which the author concentrates attention on the working of dark passions, it must be confessed that the moral purpose of the book is made more definite by this very deficiency. The most abandoned libertine could not read the volume without being thrilled into something like virtuous resolution, and the roué would find that the deep-seeing eye of the novelist had mastered the whole philosophy of that guilt of which practical roués are but childish disciples. To another class of readers, those who have theories of seduction and adultery modeled after the French school of novelists, and whom libertinism is of the brain, the volume may afford matter for very instructive and edifying contemplation; for, in truth, Hawthorne, in *The Scarlet Letter,* has utterly undermined the whole philosophy on which the French novels rest by seeing farther and deeper into the essence both of conventional and moral laws; and he has given the results of his insight, not in disquisitions and criticisms, but in representations more powerful even than those of Sue, Dumas, or George Sand.[1] He has made his guilty parties end, not as his own fancy or his own benevolent sympathies might dictate, but as the spiritual laws, lying back of all persons, dictated to him. In this respect there is hardly a novel in English literature more purely objective.

ᴗᴗᴗ

A SYMPATHY FOR THEIR SIN

Arthur Cleveland Coxe

Why has our author selected such a theme? Why, amid all the suggestive incidents of life in a wilderness; of a retreat from civilization to which, in every individual case, a thousand circumstances must have concurred to reconcile human nature with estrangement from home and country; or amid the historical connections of our history with Jesuit adventure, savage invasion, regicide outlawry, and French aggression, should the taste of Mr. Hawthome have preferred as the proper material for romance the nauseous amour of a Puritan pastor, with a frail creature of his charge, whose mind is represented as far more debauched than her body? Is it, in short, because a running undertide of filth has become as requisite to a romance as death in the fifth act to a tragedy? Is the French era actually begun in our literature? And is the flesh, as well as the world and the devil, to be henceforth dished up in fashionable novels, and discussed at parties, by spinsters and their beaux, with as unconcealed a relish as they give to the vanilla in their ice cream? We would be slow to believe it, and we hope our author would not willingly have it so, yet we honestly believe that *The Scarlet Letter* has already done not a little to degrade our literature, and to encourage social licentiousness; it has started other pens on like enterprises, and has loosed the restraint of many tongues, that have made it an apology for "the evil communications which corrupt good manners." We are painfully tempted to believe that it is a book made for the market, and that the market has made it merchantable, as they do game, by letting everybody understand

This review appeared in "The Writings of Hawthorne," *Church Review* 3 in January 1851.

1. [Eugène Sue (1804–1857), Alexandre Dumas (1824–1895), George Sand (Aurore Dupin) (1804–1876).]

that the commodity is in high condition, and smells strongly of incipient putre-faction.

We shall entirely mislead our reader if we give him to suppose that *The Scarlet Letter* is coarse in its details, or indecent in its phraseology. This very article of our own is far less suited to ears polite than any page of the romance before us; and the reason is, we call things by their right names, while the romance never hints the shocking words that belong to its things, but, like Mephistopheles, insinuates that the archfiend himself is a very tolerable sort of person, if nobody would call him Mr. Devil. We have heard of persons who could not bear the reading of some Old Testament lessons in the service of the Church: such persons would be delighted with our author's story; and damsels who shrink at the reading of the Decalogue would probably luxuriate in bathing their imagination in the crystal of its delicate sensuality. The language of our author, like patent blacking, "would not soil the whitest linen," and yet the composition itself, would suffice, if well laid on, to Ethiopize the snowiest conscience that ever sat like a swan upon that mirror of heaven, a Christian maiden's imagination. We are not sure we speak quite strong enough when we say that we would much rather listen to the coarsest scene of Goldsmith's[1] *Vicar* read aloud by a sister or daughter, than to hear from such lips the perfectly chaste language of a scene in *The Scarlet Letter,* in which a married wife and her reverend paramour, with their unfortunate offspring, are introduced as the actors, and in which the whole tendency of the conversation is to suggest a sympathy for their sin, and an anxiety that they may be able to accomplish a successful escape beyond the seas, to some country where their shameful commerce may be perpetuated. Now, in Goldsmith's story there are very coarse words, but we do not remember anything that saps the foundations of the moral sense, or that goes to create unavoidable sympathy with unrepenting sorrow, and deliberate, premeditated sin. The *Vicar of Wakefield* is sometimes coarsely virtuous, but *The Scarlet Letter* is delicately immoral.

But in Hawthorne's tale, the lady's frailty is philosophized into a natural and necessary result of the Scriptural law of marriage, which, by holding her irrevocably to her vows, as plighted to a dried up old bookworm in her silly girl-hood, is viewed as making her heart an easy victim to the adulterer. The sin of her seducer too, seems to be considered as lying not so much in the deed itself, as in his long concealment of it, and, in fact, the whole moral of the tale is given

1. [Oliver Goldsmith (1730–1774).]

in the words—"Be true—be true," as if sincerity in sin were virtue, and as if "Be clean—be clean," were not the more fitting conclusion. "The untrue man" is, in short, the hangdog of the narrative, and the unclean one is made a very interesting sort of a person, and as the two qualities are united in the hero, their composition creates the interest of his character. Shelley[2] himself never imagined a more dissolute conversation than that in which the polluted minister comforts himself with the thought, that the revenge of the injured husband is worse than his own sin in instigating it. "Thou and I never did so, Hester"—he suggests: and she responds—"never, never! What we did had *a consecration of its own*, we felt it so—we said so to each other!" This is a little too much—it carries the Bay-theory a little too far for our stomach! "Hush, Hester!" is the sickish rejoinder; and fie, Mr. Hawthorne! is the weakest token of our disgust that we can utter. The poor bemired hero and heroine of the story should not have been seen wallowing in their filth at such a rate as this.

❧❧❧

NATHANIEL HAWTHORNE

Henry James

The Scarlet Letter, in 1850, brought him immediate distinction and has probably kept its place not only as the most original of his novels, but as the most distinguished piece of prose fiction that was to spring from American soil. He had received in 1839 an appointment to a small place in the Boston Custom House, where his labors were sordid and sterile, and he had given it up in permissible weariness. He had spent in 1841 near Roxbury, Massachusetts, a few months in the cooperative community of Brook Farm, a short-lived socialistic experiment. He had married in the following year and gone to live at the Old Manse at Concord, where he remained till 1846, when, with a fresh fiscal engagement, he returned to his native town. It was in the intervals of his occupation at the Salem Custom House that *The Scarlet Letter* was written. The book has achieved the fortune of the small supreme group of novels: it has hung an ineffaceable image in the portrait gallery, the reserved inner cabinet, of literature. . . .

One of America's major novelists, Henry James (1843–1916) created fiction noted for its subtlety and psychological realism. As a literary critic, James wrote about most of the important nineteenth-century writers. In this selection, James suggests that *The Scarlet Letter* is the first distinguished novel to "spring from American soil."

2. [Percy Bysshe Shelley (1792–1822).]

In truth, for many persons his great, his most touching sign will have been his aloofness wherever he is. He is outside of everything, and an alien everywhere. He is an aesthetic solitary. His beautiful, light imagination is the wing that on the autumn evening just brushes the dusky window. It was a faculty that gave him much more a terrible sense of human abysses than a desire rashly to sound them and rise to the surface with his report. On the surface—the surface of the soul and the edge of the tragedy—he preferred to remain. He lingered, to weave his web, in the thin exterior air. This is a partial expression of his characteristic habit of dipping, of diving just for sport, into the moral world without being in the least a moralist. He had none of the heat nor of the dogmatism of that character; none of the impertinence, as we feel he would almost have held it, of any intermeddling. He never intermeddled; he was divertedly and discreetly contemplative, pausing oftenest wherever, amid prosaic aspects, there seemed most of an appeal to a sense for subtleties. But of all cynics he was the brightest and kindest, and the subtleties he spun are mere silken threads for a string of polished beads. His collection of moral mysteries is the cabinet of a dilettante.

The Custom House,
Salem, Massachusetts

THE DEVIL IN MASSACHUSETTS

Marion L. Starkey

During Martha Cory's examination, Rebecca Nurse's name had been bandied about before two or three hundred witnesses as freely as if she were already at the bar. Accordingly no one was surprised when the following day, 23 March, a warrant was issued for her arrest. What was surprising was that one outwardly so harmless should be accused of such multifarious criminal activities. All the time that Rebecca's physical part had lain helpless in bed, her Shape had flown about the country abusing nearly every girl on the roster of affliction, and adding for good measure one Sarah Bibber, a scandalmongering matron who had been hovering at the edge of "the circle" from the first, watching for her chance to be admitted as a practicing seeress.

Even this was not all. What the elder Ann Putnam had lately seen was truly dreadful; if she could prove her charges, Rebecca would be convicted not alone of sorcery but of murder.

Yet when this culprit took her stand at the bar on the morning of 24 March, there was that about her which moved even Magistrate Hathorne to compassion—and to doubt. She was, poor witch, so very old and so frail, hardly able to stand after her illness, and yet so patient as she strained her ears to grasp what was required of her. Besides, the magistrate's sister had been talking to him.

Tremulously Rebecca made her plea.

"I can say before my eternal father that I am innocent, and God will clear my innocence."

"Here is never a one in the assembly but desires it," said Hathorne, and not before had he addressed a witch so kindly. "But if you be guilty, I pray God discover you."

The testimony began. Goodman Kenny reported that once when she came to his house he had been seized with "an amazed condition"; Edward Putnam that she had tortured his niece in his presence.

"I am innocent and clear and have not been able to get out of doors these eight-nine days," said Rebecca to this. "I never afflicted no child, no, never in my life."

Who could look at Rebecca and not believe her? Hathorne gave way to his misgivings. Could not these children have made a mistake? As late as Monday Ann Putnam had not been sure that it was Rebecca whom she saw.

In her book *The Devil in Massachusetts* (1949), historian Marion L. Starkey recounts magistrate John Hathorne's examination of accused witch Rebecca Nurse, an ill and elderly woman. Hathorne (an ancestor of Nathaniel Hawthorne) was one of the most zealous magistrates in the Salem witchcraft trials, and unlike most of his fellow magistrates, never publicly repented of his part in them.

"Are you," he asked, "an innocent person relating to this witchcraft?"

He was answered immediately, unmistakably, and not by Rebecca. One of the girls fell into convulsions, and then another, and then all the girls together set up such a "hideous screech and noise" that Deodat Lawson, who had left the meetinghouse after the preliminaries to work on the Lecture Day sermon he was to deliver that afternoon, heard it at a distance and was amazed. Within the meetinghouse among the spectators there was more than amazement; there was panic. An infection of demonism was running across the whole assembly; people shrank back from the touch and look of neighbors, no longer sure who was witch and who bewitched.

Above the clamor shrilled the voice of the elder Ann Putnam. "Did you not bring the Black Man with you? Did you not bid me tempt God and die? How often have you eat and drunk to your own damnation?"

It took some time for the uproar to subside enough for Hathorne to proceed, and it was ample time for him to repent his moment of weakness.

"What do you say to them?" he demanded.

It was doubtful if Rebecca heard him. Even Parris, who had taken the office of secretary today, was finding it impossible to distinguish among the manifold cries and accusations and to set them down in order.

This Howard Pyle engraving (1892) from Mary E. Wilkins's *Giles Corey, Yeoman* illustrates an account of the 1692 trial of two accused witches in Salem, Massachusetts. The original caption read, "There is a flock of yellow-birds around her head."

"Oh, Lord, help me!" cried poor Rebecca and spread her hands helplessly. Her very gestures became an accusation against her, for the girls immediately spread theirs, and thereafter whatever move Rebecca made they duplicated. Watching the devil's choreography, the most impartial spectator could no longer credit Rebecca's plea of innocence. Words may lie, but deeds cannot. Before the very eyes of the court, she was demonstrating her witchcraft.

Hathorne, looking at her closely, saw further evidence of guilt. Would not an innocent woman weep before such a scene, as many women were weeping throughout the auditorium? Yet Rebecca was not; there was a reason for this; tears are not possible to a witch.

"It is awful for all to see these agonies," said the magistrate very slowly and distinctly to arrest the woman's dazed attention, "and you an old professor thus charged with the devil by the effects of it, and yet to see you stand with dry eyes when there are so many wet."

"You do not know my heart," whispered Rebecca.

"You would do well if you were guilty to confess. Give glory to God."

But Rebecca, frail as she was, wavering at the stand, yet possessed the Puritan's steadfastness. She would not seek the solution already discovered by Tituba; she would not confess. She was "clear as the child unborn." She had no wounds, "none but old age"; she had no familiar spirit, "none but God alone."

"Would you have me belie myself?" she asked.

Hathorne read her the most serious charge, that which the elder Ann had sworn to. It was no matter of pinching and biting; it was murder. Little children in their winding sheets had been appearing to Ann, calling her aunt, telling her dreadful things; it was Witch Nurse who had done them to death.

"What think you of this?"

"I cannot tell what to think." But the intelligence as well as the courage of Rebecca was asserting itself; she gave voice to a hypothesis which would not in the end be forgotten. "The devil may appear in my shape."

"They accuse you of hurting them, and if you think it is . . . by design, you must look on them as murderers."

But nothing could shake the denial of Rebecca. Toward noon Hathorne ordered her led away, for the meetinghouse had to be made ready for the Lecture Day sermon that Lawson was to preach in the afternoon. Parris gathered up his notes and in the peace of his study began to put them together. It was a thankless task; he was an able and diligent secretary, but there had been so many interruptions in this examination, and above all such uncontrolled commotion, that he despaired of ever getting them complete or in the right order.

☙☙

MYSTERY AND MANNERS

Flannery O'Connor

From "Some Aspects of the Grotesque in Southern Fiction"

There was a time when the average reader read a novel simply for the moral he could get out of it, and however naive that may have been, it was a good deal less naive than some of the more limited objectives he now has. Today novels

Flannery O'Connor (1925–1964) was one of the most critically acclaimed Southern fiction writers of the twentieth century. A devout Catholic, she portrays characters who must face an ultimate reality, often through a violent confrontation. The selection here is taken from her talk "Some Aspects of the Grotesque in Southern Fiction" and from an article, "The Teaching of Literature," published posthumously are considered to be entirely concerned with the social or economic or psychological forces that they will by necessity exhibit, or with those details of daily life that are for the good novelist only means to some deeper end.

Hawthorne knew his own problems and perhaps anticipated ours when he said he did not write novels, he wrote romances. Today many readers and critics have set up for the novel a kind of orthodoxy. They demand a realism of fact which may, in the end, limit rather than broaden the novel's scope. They associate the only legitimate material for long fiction with the movement of social forces, with the typical, with fidelity to the way things look and happen in normal life. Along with this usually goes a wholesale treatment of those aspects of existence that the Victorian novelist could not directly deal with. It has only been within the last five or six decades that writers have won this supposed emancipation. This was a license that opened up many possibilities for fiction, but it is always a bad day for culture when any liberty of this kind is assumed to be general. The writer has no rights at all except those he forges for himself inside his own work. We have become so flooded with sorry fiction based on unearned liberties, or on the notion that fiction must represent the typical, that in the public mind the deeper kinds of realism are less and less understandable.

The writer who writes within what might be called the modern romance tradition may not be writing novels which in all respects partake of a novelistic orthodoxy; but as long as these works have vitality, as long as they present something that is alive, however eccentric its life may seem to the general reader, then they have to be dealt with; and they have to be dealt with on their own terms.

From "The Teaching of Literature"

In the act of writing, one sees that the way a thing is made controls and is inseparable from the whole meaning of it. The form of a story gives it meaning which any other form would change, and unless the student is able, in some degree, to apprehend the form, he will never apprehend anything else about the work, except what is extrinsic to it as literature.

The result of the proper study of a novel should be contemplation of the mystery embodied in it, but this is a contemplation of the mystery in the whole work and not of some proposition or paraphrase. It is not the tracking down of an expressible moral or statement about life. An English teacher that I knew once asked her students what the moral of *The Scarlet Letter* was, and one answer she got was the moral of *The Scarlet Letter* was, think twice before you commit adultery.

Many students are made to feel that if they can dive deep into a piece of fiction and come up with so edifying a proposition as this, their effort has not been in vain.

I think, to judge from what the nation reads, that most of our effort in the teaching of literature has been in vain, and I think that this is even more apparent when we listen to what people demand of the novelist. If people don't know what they get, they at least know what they want. Possibly the question most often asked these days about modern fiction is why do we keep on getting novels about freaks and poor people, engaged always in some violent, destructive action, when actually, in this country, we are rich and strong and democratic and the man in the street is possessed of a general good will which overflows in all directions.

I think that this kind of question is only one of many attempts, unconscious perhaps, to separate mystery from manners in fiction, and thereby to make it more palatable to the modern taste. The novelist is asked to begin with an examination of statistics rather than with an examination of conscience. Or if he must examine his conscience, he is asked to do so in the light of statistics. I'm afraid, though, that this is not the way the novelist uses his eyes. For him, judgment is implicit in the act of seeing. His vision cannot be detached from his moral sense.

Readers have got somewhat out of the habit of feeling that they have to drain off a statable moral from a novel. Now they feel they have to drain off a statable social theory that will make life more worth living. What they wish to eliminate from fiction, at all costs, is the mystery that James foresaw the loss of. The storyteller must render what he sees and not what he thinks he ought to see, but this doesn't mean that he can't be, or that he isn't, a moralist in the sense proper to him.

Glossary of Literary Terms

allegory A device in which characters and events stand for abstract ideas, principles, or forces, so that the literal situation suggests a deeper symbolic meaning.

alliteration The repetition of identical or nearly identical sounds at the beginning of consecutive or nearby words.

allusion A reference to a person, place, thing, or event, historical or fictional, that suggests a wider frame of reference or greater depth of meaning.

ambiguity A situation expressed in such a way as to allow more than one possible interpretation.

climax The point of greatest intensity or complication in a narrative; the turning point in a plot or dramatic action.

connotation The ideas and feelings commonly associated with or suggested by a word.

elegy A formal and sustained lament on the death of a particular person (adj., elegiac).

epiphany A moment of sudden insight or enlightenment that provides a character with new understanding about himself or herself or about a situation.

foreshadowing An indirect suggestion or clues that predict events yet to unfold in a story.

hyperbole A figure of speech that uses exaggeration for emphasis or effect and can also reveal aspects of a character or situation that are not directly stated.

imagery The sensory details in a written work, both literal and figurative, that create vivid impressions and emotional suggestions.

irony The contrast between what is directly relayed (through speech or description) and what is actually meant, or a state of affairs that is the opposite of what is expected.

metaphor A figure of speech that involves an implied or direct comparison between two relatively unlike things.

mood The atmosphere that is created by the author's choice of details and the words used to present them.

motivation The reasoning or emotion that drives a character's actions.

narrative An account or story of actual or fictional events.

novel A long, fictional narrative in prose.

objective correlative A term coined by T. S. Eliot to describe a set of objects, a chain of events, or a situation that evokes a particular emotion.

paradox An apparent contradiction that is often true under examination.

personification A figure of speech in which human characteristics are assigned to nonhuman things.

point of view The perspective from which a story is told, such as first person, third-person limited, and third-person omniscient.

protagonist The central character around which the story revolves.

rhetoric The art of persuasion; the use of specific devices to achieve the intellectual and emotional effects that will persuade an audience.

romance A fictional narrative that features unusual characters, exotic locations, and/or improbable and unrealistic events.

setting When and where a story takes place, including aspects of history, geography, season, social circumstances, and atmosphere.

simile A comparison between two unlike things using the word *like* or *as*.

symbol Something that is itself and also stands for something else.

syntax The combination of words into phrases, clauses, and sentences.

theme A central idea in a literary work.

tone The attitude or feeling that pervades a given work, as determined by word choice, style, imagery, connotation, sound, and rhythm.

understatement A figure of speech that uses restraint or indifference to achieve irony or rhetorical effect.

Selected Bibliography

Brooks, Van Wyck. *The Flowering of New England, 1815–1865.* New York: E. P. Dutton, 1940; Boston: Houghton Mifflin, 1981.

Chase, Richard Volney. "Hawthorne and the Limits of Romance." In *The American Novel and Its Tradition.* Garden City, New York: Doubleday, 1957.

Cowley, Malcolm, ed. *The Portable Nathaniel Hawthorne.* Rev. and exp. ed. New York: Penguin, 1977.

Demos, John Putnam. *Entertaining Satan: Witchcraft and the Culture of Early New England.* New York: Oxford University Press, 1982.

Hoffman, Daniel. "Hawthorne." In *Form and Fable in American Fiction.* New York: Oxford University Press, 1961; Charlottesville: University Press of Virginia, 1994.

Lawrence, D. H. *Studies in Classic American Literature.* New York: Thomas Selzer, 1923; New York: Penguin, 1977.

Lewis, R. W. B. *The American Adam: Innocence, Tragedy, and Tradition in the Nineteenth Century.* Chicago: University of Chicago Press, 1955.

Matthiessen, F. O. *American Renaissance: Art and Expression in the Age of Emerson and Whitman.* New York: Oxford University Press, 1941.

McIntosh, James, ed. *Nathaniel Hawthorne's Tales: Authoritative Texts, Background, Criticism.* New York: W. W. Norton, 1987.

Mellow, James R. *Nathaniel Hawthorne in His Times.* Baltimore: Johns Hopkins University Press, 1980.

Miller, Edwin Haviland. *Salem Is My Dwelling Place: A Life of Nathaniel Hawthorne.* Iowa City: University of Iowa Press, 1991.

Van Doren, Mark. *Nathaniel Hawthorne.* New York: William Sloane, 1949.

Acknowledgments

All possible care has been taken to trace ownership and secure permission for each selection in this book. The Great Books Foundation wishes to thank the following authors, publishers, and representatives for permission to reprint copyrighted material:

The Diary of Michael Wigglesworth, from THE DIARY OF MICHAEL WIGGLESWORTH: 1653–1657, edited by Edmund S. Morgan. Copyright 1946 by Edmund S. Morgan. Reprinted by permission of Edmund S. Morgan.

Christ's Fidelity, from "Christ's Fidelity the Only Shield Against Satan's Malignity," by Deodat Lawson, from SALEM-VILLAGE WITCHCRAFT: A DOCUMENTARY RECORD OF LOCAL CONFLICT IN COLONIAL NEW ENGLAND, edited by Paul Boyer and Stephen Nissenbaum. Copyright 1972 by Wadsworth Publishing Co., Inc.; new edition copyright 1993 by Paul Boyer and Stephen Nissenbaum. Reprinted by permission of Northeastern University Press, Boston.

The Devil in Massachusetts, from THE DEVIL IN MASSACHUSETTS, by Marion L. Starkey. Copyright 1949 by Marion L. Starkey. Reprinted by permission of Curtis Brown, Ltd.

Mystery and Manners, excerpted from "Some Aspects of the Grotesque in Southern Fiction" and "The Teaching of Literature," from MYSTERY AND MANNERS, by Flannery O'Connor. Copyright 1969 by the estate of Mary Flannery O'Connor. Reprinted by permission of Farrar, Straus and Giroux, LLC.

Photo and Art Credits

ii "The Rose," wood engraving by Barry Moser. From *The Scarlet Letter*, by Nathaniel Hawthorne, designed and illustrated by Barry Moser, published by Pennyroyal Press, 1984. **8** *Nathaniel Hawthorne*, by Charles Osgood, 1840, oil on canvas. Courtesy of the Peabody Essex Museum, Salem, Massachusetts. Gift of Richard Clarke Manning, 1933. **11** Photograph of Una, Julian, and Rose Hawthorne by Silsbee and Case, circa 1862. Courtesy of the Peabody Essex Museum, Salem, Massachusetts. **12** *Brook Farm*, oil on panel by Josiah Wolcott, 1844. Courtesy of the Massachusetts Historical Society. **15** © Bettmann/CORBIS. **17** The Wayside. Courtesy of the Concord Free Public Library. **18** Paul Strand: *Church on a Hill, Northern Vermont, 1945.* © 1950 Aperture Foundation, Inc., Paul Strand Archive. **31** Paul Strand: *Steeple, Northern Vermont, 1945.* © 1950 Aperture Foundation, Inc., Paul Strand Archive. **34** Paul Strand: *Spruce and Lichen, Maine, 1945.* © 1950 Aperture Foundation, Inc., Paul Strand Archive. **49** © Chinch Gryniewicz; Ecoscene/CORBIS. **52** "Hester at Her Needle," wood engraving by Barry Moser. From *The Scarlet Letter*, by Nathaniel Hawthorne, designed and illustrated by Barry Moser, published by Pennyroyal Press, 1984. **68** "Arthur Dimmesdale," wood engraving by Barry Moser. From *The Scarlet Letter*, by Nathaniel Hawthorne, designed and illustrated by Barry Moser, published by Pennyroyal Press, 1984. **94** "A," ink drawing by Yvette Rutledge. From *The Scarlet Letter*, by Nathaniel Hawthorne, designed and illustrated by Barry Moser, published by Pennyroyal Press, 1984. **105** "Dimmesdale with the Sign of Sin," wood engraving by Barry Moser. From *The Scarlet Letter*, by Nathaniel Hawthorne, designed and illustrated by Barry Moser, published by Pennyroyal Press, 1984. **106** "Pearl with Bouquet of Wildflowers," wood engraving by Barry Moser. From *The Scarlet Letter*, by Nathaniel Hawthorne, designed and illustrated by Barry Moser, published by Pennyroyal Press, 1984. **111** Paul Strand: *"Memento Mori," Tombstone, Vermont, 1946.* © 1950 Aperture Foundation, Inc., Paul Strand Archive. **112** *Mrs. Elizabeth Freake and Baby Mary*, by Anonymous, oil on canvas. Courtesy of Worcester Art Museum, Worcester, Massachusetts, gift of Mr. and Mrs. Albert W. Rice. **114 (t)** © Bettmann/CORBIS. **115 (t)** © Michael Freeman. **115 (c)** © G. E. Kidder Smith/CORBIS. **115 (b, r)** Gloves belonging to Leverett, circa 1640–1650. Photo by Jeffery Dykes. Courtesy of the Peabody Essex Museum, Salem, Massachusetts. **117** Paul Strand: *"Death the Victor," Tombstone, Vermont, 1946.* © 1950 Aperture Foundation, Inc., Paul Strand Archive. **121** Courtesy of the Rare Book and Special Collections Library, University of Sydney. **123** © CORBIS **126** © Bettmann/CORBIS. **128** © Bettmann/CORBIS. **132** © Bettmann/CORBIS. **134** © Bettman/CORBIS. **136 (t, l)** Hulton | Archive by Getty Images. **136 (b)** Hulton | Archive by Getty Images. **137 (b, l)** © CORBIS SYGMA. **137 (b, r)** © Michal Daniel. **144** © Bettmann/CORBIS.